If It Gets Quiet Later On, I Will Make a Display

NICK THRAN

NIGHTWOOD EDITIONS

Nightwood Editions
P.O. Box 1779
Gibsons, BC VON 1VO
Canada
www.nightwoodeditions.com

COVER DESIGN: Anna Comfort O'Keeffe
TYPESETTING: Carleton Wilson

Nightwood Editions acknowledges the support of the Canada Council for the Arts,
the Government of Canada, and the Province of British Columbia through the BC Arts Council.

This book has been produced on 100% post-consumer recycled, ancient-forest-free paper,
processed chlorine-free and printed with vegetable-based dyes.

Printed and bound in Canada.

LIBRARY AND ARCHIVES CANADA CATALOGUING IN PUBLICATION

Title: If it gets quiet later on, I will make a display / Nick Thran.
Names: Thran, Nick, 1980- author.
Description: Essays, stories, and poems.
Identifiers: Canadiana (print) 20220481725 | Canadiana (ebook) 20220481741 |
ISBN 9780889714489 (softcover) | ISBN 9780889714496 (EPUB)
Classification: LCC PS8639.H73 I4 2023 | DDC C811/.6—dc23

For Abigail.

~&

And for Stan Dragland (1942–2022), bricoleur.
I had been looking forward to sharing this book with you.

We're inside the bookstore before it's open.

Rumours of the great
all-knowing egg
have thus far proven false.

They've published weeds
and trees
and flowers.

We've walked
the dark aisles of the world
without a working thesis.

There is no quiet
quite like this.

It has scratched its way into the walls.

It will not be sold
or be mastered.

CONTENTS

I

IF IT GETS QUIET LATER ON, I WILL MAKE A DISPLAY

To live in the micro-city of Fredericton and ignore the presence of trees would be like living in Manhattan and pretending there are no people. Fredericton is sometimes referred to as the City of Stately Elms. When architects propose new infrastructure requiring one or more of those elms to be removed, many of us petition and protest. When boreal disease ravages our streetside givers of shade, chainsaws purchased with taxpayer dollars are quick to show their teeth. Some of us step out of our doorways to idle before the stumps, shaking our heads partly to acknowledge one another, partly to eulogize. It is something of the procession of tree mourners "in the streets, or the woodland aisles," that Henry David Thoreau lamented did not exist whenever a tree was felled near Walden Pond.

The bookstore where I work part-time has included among its top sellers in recent years *The Great Trees of New Brunswick*, *Forest Bathing*, *The Overstory* and *The Hidden Life of Trees*. Like other reading communities across the country, we are fascinated by the mycorrhizal network, a network now commonly known as the wood wide web. Scientists like Canadian Suzanne Simard have been able to prove what the local Wolastoqiyik communities have understood for longer than the settlers have been on this land: that trees ("tree people") communicate with one another, and with other species.

Simard, in *Finding the Mother Tree*, offers an expansive theory of mappable fungal networks, communication between trees in order to strengthen bonds, trade sugars, warn of attack, bind at the deeper roots. It seems that the more mythological presences of trees in fables and religion couple with Indigenous knowledge and Western science that proves boreal sentience and cooperation, the more our imaginations are engaged with the world out here, in the middle of what is not nowhere, because we count among the population all of those whom the Great Spirit's helper Koluskap called, in Wolastoqiyik legend, the Standing Ones.

A FEW YEARS AGO, I lived in New York City. I didn't know much about visual art, but I knew the Armory Show in Manhattan was a place to go see a lot of it because Frank O'Hara references the show toward the end of his poem "A Step Away from Them":

> And one has eaten and one walks,
> past the magazines with nudes
> and the posters for BULLFIGHT and
> the Manhattan Storage Warehouse,
> which they'll soon tear down. I
> used to think they had the Armory
> Show there.

I did "art" in New York like I did all other things: went in green, and binged. I loved leaving an afternoon at the galleries in a sort of beatific trance, understanding that even the escalators and coffee carts were miracles of ingenuity, gleaming with aesthetic pleasures.

But there was so much art at the Armory Show, even I had to admit it was tiring me out. So many paintings and sculptures crammed into every dealer's small display space. It was a relief, then, to turn the corner into a makeshift room with three complete walls and a partial fourth, to suddenly find myself among (deep, recollecting breath) a series of towering, silent, black and white photographs of trees.

You can picture these trees without too much description: nostalgic black and white undertones to their grains and knots, viewer face to face with all of the subtle and not-so-subtle variations of the bark. Big, vertical images taken with something called a banquet camera. Think of the great North American character studies in photography by Nan Goldin or Walker Evans—technical attributes applied not to people, but to trees.

To get that much physical space at an international art fair like the Armory, I figured you had to be a pretty big deal. So I was surprised, swanning through Sackville (a tiny university town two hours outside of Fredericton) a few years later, when my wife Sue and I ran into her old friend Thaddeus, who was the photographer responsible for those towering trees in the Armory Show. On this particular evening he was selling movie tickets for the town's weekly film club, held in a cavernous vestige of modernism called the Vogue Cinema. She asked him what he'd been up to for the past twenty years. The silver-bearded photographer—who headed the fine arts department of the local university, published numerous catalogues and sold his artwork to dealers around the world—simply shrugged, a roll of red raffle tickets waving in one of his hands. "Oh, you know, I'm still here."

SUE WENT OUT to Fredericton early in order to scout for our first home. She settled on a mid-twentieth-century house not too far from the university where she had been hired to work. "Look at this," she typed along with the pictures. "The yard is full of all of these huge and beautiful trees!"

I had to admit it looked promising, and agreed, without visiting, to the purchase.

For the following three years these huge and beautiful trees became the wires through which I transmitted every anxiety and frustration I was feeling about adjusting to my new environment, to my new roles as a homemaker and the caretaker of a house on a semi-forested plot of land. The branches, before we had arborists in to scale them back, scratched at the new shingles of the roof, waking me most nights. Those same branches would also provide walkways for squirrels and mice to travel from the ground to the warmth of our attic, and during the night I seemed, among my household of three, to be the only one tuned to the music of their tiny claws scraping against the wood. The soffits would tear. Branches had to be cleared from the lawn after every storm. A pileated woodpecker came pecking, signalling the imminent death of one white birch near the deck. During some high winds, a spruce was uprooted in the neighbours' yard, falling over and destroying their shed, confirming every fear of impending calamity that had been festering in my brain. One day I noticed that a pin cherry in our yard had begun reclining into the wrestling ropes of black power lines above the back fence. Another day I noticed a birch had acquired a rusty red stain mid-trunk, and black crow's toes for roots. Arborists told us that the deadfall hanging from the top of another grey birch had to be trimmed, lest it fall to the driveway and crush the car. Worst was the great maple leaning over our child's room, a maple that, to this day, arborists continue to assure me is strong, healthy, and just leaning that way to catch a bit more of the afternoon sun.

What had begun as a mix of typical domestic loneliness, fear and an anxiety over the new and, to me, unnatural concept of home ownership was beginning to disguise itself as an outright animosity toward nature. Once my child started school, I had to get some kind of job downtown among other people if I hoped to stay rooted to the ground.

I work there on Sunday afternoons, alone. I get a few customers from twelve to three. Then things get quiet, Walden Pond quiet. My main task during these last couple of hours is to make the displays on the tabletops and the displays in the windows that face out to the street.

THIS IS MY second multi-year stint as a bookseller. My first foray into bookselling occurred in Toronto, where I fluctuated between part- to full-time positions for about four years. Before becoming a bookseller I had been working in a busy downtown boutique hotel as a utility-knife bellhop: parking cars, carrying suitcases, making restaurant reservations. As I was new to the city, the job at the hotel appealed to my desire to feel inside the vascular tissue of the metropolis. At the same time, it provided me with enough of a buffer between myself and other people that I never really needed to make myself known. I was there to deliver things, to accommodate, to please.

For a year and a half I stood out front under the hotel's awning on Bloor Street, with a view of the Royal Ontario Museum's refracted, modern, crystallized awning and the rich red brick facade of the Opera House. From three in the afternoon to eleven at night I would perform a set of sometimes simple, sometimes difficult and occasionally degrading tasks. (One of the worst of these was scraping gum off the sole of a slightly embarrassed foreign diplomat's shoe at the behest of his angry and belligerent host.) After my shift ended, I would walk west to the student bars in the Annex, my pockets stuffed with five, ten and twenty dollar bills. Those bars were closest to my one-room accommodation in a boarding house shared with nine other men. It was in a central location, cost three hundred a month and had a smell that reminded me of my grandfather. On a good night I'd stumble home after last call, but more often than not I'd wander farther downtown to the booze cans and after-hours clubs located in the basements and repurposed parking lots of the city's core. What happened after that is mostly lost. I'd wake up at noon, my pockets empty, the ashtray beside me on the bed often still smouldering. I'd assess my remaining cigarette inventory, light one up if one was left, shower and dress, grab a coffee and a chocolate chip muffin at my nearby Tim Hortons, make the thirty-minute walk over to the hotel for a late cafeteria lunch before the start of my shift, and start the routine all over again.

I probably could have spent a few more years in this way if I hadn't wanted to write a book of poems. I applied to a month-long poetry workshop across the country, at the Banff Centre. I got in. Hotel management begrudgingly gave me the time off work. For a month I could replace those eight hours at the hotel with eight hours to read and write.

Returning to Toronto from those mountains, I soon found myself in the middle of an August heat wave. I had been tasked, during checkout, with moving forty suitcases down to the front entrance. The suitcases belonged to an oil oligarch and his family. My colleagues who had checked him in warned me: this was going to be hell. Each suitcase might as well have been full of books. The handles were all broken, and rumour had it the unionized airport luggage crew had refused, on legal grounds, to remove these cases from the plane. The work took about an hour. The oligarch's assistant was hard to find. I felt my recurring back pain flare as I searched him out. My uniform was soaked in sweat, though you could hardly tell, given that the uniforms were a purposely thick and sweat-disguising forest green. When I did find the assistant, he reluctantly peeled off a single twenty-dollar bill, and I walked to the back office and told the manager that this was to be my last shift at the hotel. The other bellhops commiserated with me, of course, but these were men with families to feed, gifts to send to mothers and fathers in other countries, and mortgages to pay on apartments and houses. These were men who didn't seem to follow their anger or exhaustion to the end of the line in the way I did, who understood that the flow of oligarchs, actors and businessmen was ongoing, but with moments of exhalation; that no matter what happened while any individual was here, there would be that moment of peace when they'd eventually leave.

COOL CLOUDS ON A DRIVE

Part burnt conifers, part salmon bellies.
            The intersection where
ten lanes converge on a dog's breakfast
has been dug up. A cone. Another cone.
            A cone. River that,
            albeit beautiful to behold,
means we've gone too far.
            Long curve back
            toward downtown.
            Summer rerun of *Ideas*,
            a loud Irish jug band
in the bandshell serenading
the field of box-store folding chairs. Pause
            at a green light,
            the driver ahead in a smartphone bow
holding up the lane. Bit of excess speed
through a stretch of colonial homes where the sprinklers
sing in that Ageean, *A Death in the Family* way.
            But we weren't really late.
            We couldn't be late.
We were just seeing the clouds from all sides.

BOOK IT

Book It had been an institution on Main Street for thirty years, thriving when Main Street was still the place to be downtown, on foot, after five p.m. Best little restaurants, owned by immigrant families from all over the world. The best bars, run by upstart kids with dyed hair and coke nails. Record stores. Sex shops. Used books. New books. People would come down from the towers like bats at dusk, browse around the store before or after drinks, sometimes before *and* after drinks. Then the big boxes and chain restaurants came in, and the landlords, with dollar signs in their eyes, started indiscriminately jacking the rent, hoping to land a Sapling Electronics or Thai Fry Supreme on their ground floors. Then the jobs in the buildings themselves all blurred into an omnivorous cell of energy extraction, tech and speculative wealth. Only the twenty-four-hour 200K suits could afford to live there, and all they really seemed to want to do was to doomscroll on their phones over bowl after bowl of same-every-time pad thai.

Well, that was only part of the story. Book It hung on for so long because it had two shelves that, no matter the changes, mattered: books with pictures of people fucking, and books with the words of various gods. The dance of the customer every evening usually took one of two forms: the customers who wanted coffee table books of people fucking would come in and make an exaggerated show of their initial presence. A cursory two- to three-minute browse of the other 95 percent of the shelf space would occur, but usually only so far as the new arrivals and discount tables. Then they would be there, a metre away from the register, but miles away in their quiet, browsing the oversized pages of fists in orifices, of leather, of clenched teeth, of blazing eyes. This one. This one... Some evenings two or three purchases of this kind accounted for everything on the tally. But as the world wide web got wilder, and the noise-cancelling headphones got better, even the life on that shelf started to slow.

The people who wanted the words of gods always knew exactly where they were in the store, and made no show of pretending to be interested in any Ishiguro or Munro. Mostly they came in, walked right across the front of the register to the shelf with the Bibles, the Qurans, the Bhagavad Gitas, barely acknowledging G's presence, barely acknowledging the neighbouring section of pleasure, pain and pleasures in pain. They bought one book and one book only. Or they stole the book if you weren't careful. No shelf simultaneously accounted for more sales and more lost inventory.

But the time had come now to reckon with what had been evident for a long time. Neither sex nor religion could keep the booksellers where they were. The owner laid out the deal for G in plain terms. The new and sudden rent increase was criminal, and they were going to fight the landlord like the bookish pirates they were. A team of twelve people would appear in the store at midnight the following Monday, hydrated and ready to box up everything in the store, to pull posters from walls, etc. At two a.m. a truck would appear outside with its hazards on. They'd load the boxes in quickly, then they'd drive to Book It's flagship location in the Riverpath district. The hours of that store would be pushed later into the night, and as the longest-tenured member of staff, G would get those hours if he wanted them. The Main Street store was closed.

G *did* want those hours. He needed them. The evening of the move was a thrill. They were moving the inventory they already owned, from a neighbourhood that no longer wanted them, so it wasn't a heist (not exactly). But to be up late with a team of part-timers and friends of staff, working up a sweat over a two-hour period under the cover of night, it felt something like those days when he'd lock up the store on a summer evening to go talk with his co-workers about the new Bernadette Mayer over dollar beers at the Albion Moonlight, occasionally getting drunk enough to let their guards down and go dancing at the Mutual Aid, where all people and all bodies were celebrated, where the booksellers would sometimes surprise themselves with their moves.

Boxing the books, they started from the top shelves, two people per section. Names of novelists, historians and philosophers that he hadn't thought about in five, ten years flashed before his eyes. The tape guns stretched out and bit down. As the truck drove off he felt the wind on his long but thinning hair, and promised he would take the new gig, its reduced hours and late nights, with less cynicism, with more gratitude. He would move lightly through the entire store, dusting off old bits of knowledge, and put the two heavy shelves that had anchored him here for so long out of mind, maybe for good.

———❧———

The customers in the Riverpath location were smarter than he was, that was clear to him almost right away. They stayed for a long time, and they bought giant, varied piles of both hardcovers and paperbacks. They bought new works by Indigenous authors who were decolonizing the very ideas of genre; they bought graphic novels with anxious narrators upfront about every aspect of their mental health; they bought anti-racist books and books about climate disaster; they bought field guides celebrating moths and wildflowers and they bought novels whose speakers had inner monologues so cruel that they would make the sci-fi and horror writers he grew up reading cringe.

It was good that his hours were reduced, because he needed the time to read if he was going to be of any service. The long train ride from home helped. So did the daylight hours. He listened for months to the customers describing the books that excited them.

His co-workers were as smart as the customers. All were younger than him and regarded G with suspicion, sometimes with open disdain. Eventually, a few let their guards down. Eventually, he made a couple of friends.

Was there any value in the Beats, the potboilers and the deconstructionists he grew up reading? Sure. But that was a chapter in a book of many chapters. For five years he had sold nothing but sex and God, and now G had the chance to sell things that he could barely articulate the value of. Maybe this was the real work of a bookseller. People selling cars knew what would top out at the highest highway speed, what engine was best for the starts and stops. People selling groceries knew where both the carrots and the cupcakes were. But he would always know, at best, only 5 percent of whatever Book It had in stock. That thought stirred something in G, somewhere right between belonging and desire.

A JOHN ASHBERY REMEMBRANCE DAY

A call came into the shop from someone looking for your *Girls on the Run*.

We didn't have the book.

Could not have been expected to have the book.

But I offered to order the hardcover edition, which was still in print,

also suggested *Notes from the Air*,

and one of the Library of America collected volumes

which would include *Girls on the Run* in its entirety,

providing the customer with more of the work for a small mark-up in price.

The t-shirt I was wearing had a crude drawing of your face—a gift that my
wife had ordered online.

The poppy on my sweater looked pinned to your hair.

I didn't tell the customer I was wearing the shirt.

Instead I wrote it here,

just a little bit high on the feeling of being of use.

SMALL TALK

Might have taken a snow day, but I like
opening the bookstore. Even those heavy-legged

steps there. Order a takeaway coffee extra hot,
so after I shovel the sidewalk, put out the OPEN sign,

the cup will still be warm. Flick on the switches
for five afternoon hours of indoor light

in which I see nine customers
and sell four greeting cards, one collection

of personal essays, one YA novel, one self-
help book about getting rid of the habits

"that minimize the self." I love making the themed
(albeit only broadly associative) tabletop

displays. This one, called "Small Talk," includes
a book about the life of cells, something about knitting

a "mini cosmos," the history of the mosquito,
a pocket dictionary of word origins ... The coffee is

still warm. I add a book about designing terrariums,
a discussion of "micro-trends," a debut work of fiction

called *That Tiny Life.*
I mentally compose this micro-fiction

where a cup of coffee stays warm for an entire day
and the protagonist tells this to everyone

who comes into the store. Workshop the plot
by snow-shovel blade with a curious pigeon

who explains they come from a great line
of messengers, is out of work but still alive

thanks to the smokestacks piping
from the tops of the buildings

as heat reads its shivering wings.
Exchange tips about kicking the nicotine habit,

what the gentlest kinds of road salt are—
the coffee is still warm.

Meanwhile Kalpna is constructing paper swans
for a window on Queen Street. Eiko,

after a long flight back from Kyoto
is reading a poem about jet lag in an overstuffed chair

at the Community Bookstore on Seventh Ave.
John is stacking copies of the *Bakka Anthology*

on a table on Harbord Street, in the store named
for "the weeper who mourns for all mankind."

Meaghan phones businesses around Sainte-Catherine
to see who might repair the Argo's shattered glass.

Hsiang guards the tower full of books
described as "near and far at the same time"

in a poem by Jorge, who, according to Alberto,
ordered bland food at supper so that the meal

would not distract the diners from the talk.
I love the visible edges of the tables,

the shelves. Try to cultivate an understanding
of the movements of a browser's voice and eyes,

when it's time to stop talking,
to leave them wandering, to rearrange

my own voice in accordance with new arrivals,
cold coffee, with the sun going down every day

like a grand idea put off as evening sorts out the stars
from streetlights, snow from the moving cars.

LIBRERÍA GLORIA FUERTES

The store is tucked away in the Recoletos, the dense cultural hub of central Madrid. The neighbourhood is home to the National Library, to touchstone booksellers like the outdoor San Ginés Bookshop (strategically placed just down from the iconic Chocolatería), Casa del Libro (which caters to the Spanish general reader), Librería Desperate Literature (which caters to visiting American and British literati), specialty bookstores like Librería Miguel Miranda (antiques) and Librería Mujeres (feminism).

C was an American, a generalist, a feminist, a lover of chocolate and a person with sometimes antiquated tastes in literature. Yet the shop she loved most was this modest one sandwiched between a shoe store and a pharmacy, original glass on the windows, its regal blue awning with barely legible gold cursive: Librería Gloria Fuertes, named after the most well-regarded female poet from the postwar generation of 1950. In fact, as far as an anthology of Spanish poetry in English from 1900–1975 she'd found in a used bookstore back in Pennsylvania was concerned, Gloria was the *only* female poet regarded by the establishment at all. She'd been allotted thirteen scant pages in an anthology of over five hundred. The rest of the poets in the anthology were men. And to add more salt, Fuertes had been translated by a well-known male American poet who, working in a car factory for a couple of years, felt entitled to speak on behalf of the working classes for the rest of his career.

Through a number of obstacles, Gloria Fuertes wrote poems. She wrote poems through a childhood with parents who did not support her writing, through the Spanish Civil War that could have taken her life, through the regime of Franco with its repressive ideas about women's place in society, through her clandestine lesbian relationships, through the career in children's literature that could have infantilized and diminished her reputation. Through all of this, Gloria Fuertes wrote these powerful poems, transmissible even in English, that first planted the seed of this gap year in Spain in C's mind:

> When sheep pass, they pass over me,
> and perched on my fingers, the sparrows eat,
> the ants think I'm earth,
> and men think I'm nothing.

A store named after a touchstone poet was, for C, a kind of sign. She entered, hoping they might have a section of Spanish poets translated into English. They did not. What they did have was more books per square inch then she had ever seen. Shelves of Spanish cedar went from the floor right to where the walls met the ceiling. The complete collections from the flagship poetry publishing houses of Spain were here, both of which did an extraordinary job of bringing the world of English-language poetry into Spanish. Established figures like Anne Carson and John Ashbery, but also younger contemporaries, Sarah Holland-Batt from Australia, Morgan Parker from the United States. Nothing like this place existed back home, and she almost started to cry upon entering, particularly when she turned a corner to a section simply called: *los pasados por alto*, which appeared to feature Spanish poets of the African diaspora, gender-queer poets of Spain and other places in Europe, and Spanish women, not just those being published now, but those published in the fifties and sixties, back when Gloria Fuertes was, according to the almost comically named editor Hardie St. Martin, the only female Spanish poet alive worth orbiting the idea of "best."

The bookseller, a woman in her fifties, seemed to register the experience C was having, gazing at the shelves. She brought C a paper cup filled with tea poured from a thermos she kept at the cash register. She put her hand on C's shoulder, and began to speak. C had no idea what she was saying. Told her so, in English, at the first sign of a pause. But the bookseller kept speaking to her anyway, not registering even the slightest discomfort at C's lack of comprehension. Eventually the bookseller urged C to continue walking around the store, which she did, pulling the inscrutable texts of *los pasados de alto* from the shelf and admiring their covers, idly flipping and imagining there was a kind of vellum over each page that she would one day be able to remove.

C visited the store each day for six days after that. Each day she was greeted with a cup of tea and a one-sided conversation from the bookseller. One night, walking to her one-room sublet after visiting an exhibit on postwar architecture in Salamanca at the Reina Sofia, she got the idea that she would drop her resume off the next day at the Librería Gloria Fuertes. She'd worked at her local Barnes & Noble in Harrisburg the previous summer, and though she was not able to speak Spanish with any fluency, she thought perhaps she could alphabetize, shelve, dust—do the kinds of domestic work required to keep a store like that in shape. She knew that her chances would be zero, and seemed to double down on this by bringing an English copy of her CV, not wanting to advertise herself as anything other than the *extranjera* that she was.

C was hired on the following Monday. She showed up for work, was greeted with tea, and directed toward a stack of new philosophy books that needed shelving. True to what C had imagined, she mostly dusted, mopped, shelved and carefully wiped the antique glass windows with a warm, damp cloth. Nevertheless, customers *would* approach her. Each time her jaw muscles clenched as she prepared for the inevitable awkwardness, but each time, perhaps high on the generosity of spirit the store itself seemed to impart, the customers would simply go on talking and gesturing with their hands, fully animated, as if her missives of incomprehension were the most interesting things they'd ever heard.

Eventually C grew accustomed to these interactions, even comfortable. One day, after a long, one-sided conversation with an older gentleman in a caftan, she made the bold move of selecting a random title off the shelf, which turned out to be a short historical poem from thirteenth-century Córdoba in Spanish translation, the *Elegy to al-Andalus* by Abu al-Baqa ar-Rundi. The man looked at the book for a moment, and after a nerve-wracking couple of seconds, brought it to his chest and smiled, thanking C for the recommendation.

C continued in this manner for the next few weeks, recommending books to customers at random. Each instance was met with gratitude. The bookseller watched C at work, finished her thermos of tea and dutifully rang each purchase through. The bookseller knew every Fuertes poem by heart. Sometimes, when the store was empty, she and C would be reciting the same lines—C in English translation, the bookseller in the original Spanish. But this was done in their own minds, independently of one another. So how would the other know?

> I spent my whole childhood wanting
> to lean out and see what could be seen
> from the windows that were not there.

Of course, in time, C's Spanish would improve. She would begin to understand a lot more of what was being said around her: she listened dutifully as the bookseller complained at length about her son, who worked in speculative finance, who was draining the education system with some intricate loopholes and fine print (while at the same time personally financing his mother's store through the more difficult months). She fielded complaints from customers about what was or wasn't in stock. Eventually, titles started to take shape in C's mind, as did section headings like *the overlooked*, then full sentences on the dust jackets and, finally, full paragraphs inside of the many books. The spell she'd been under for a few months took the form of a regular job, and, as the mists cleared, her recommendations to customers didn't always land with the same sense of rightness. But at night she would cart a couple of the books home under her arm (which the owner allowed, provided they were returned in pristine condition) and began to wrest an idea of Spanish literature away from the editors of the New York publishing houses, from her own monolingual upbringing in an increasingly fascist United States, from the added gates and gatekeepers between her and this country, Spain, that was beginning to resemble a place she might call home, the place where the window was.

II

IF IT GETS QUIET LATER ON, I WILL MAKE A DISPLAY

The August heat wave broke, and I was a week or so without a job. A poet friend worked at a local bookstore in Bloor West Village. As a poetry editor for a small Canadian press, he wanted to see my manuscript to print, and thought it wise that I adjust my life in whatever ways I could to make that happen. I talked with him over lunch and he got me an interview with his store manager. This first bookstore was a few subway stations west of my back pains and blackouts. I worked there mostly during the late afternoons and into the evenings, not so different from my hotel shifts. But instead of disposable income, at the end of the day I left with books: free advance reading copies, books sold at a 40 percent staff discount should I want to make them mine. A widely diverse forest of information and artistry was at my fingertips, and mostly books I wouldn't have sought out otherwise. I had done an undergraduate degree in English. I had taken poetry workshops. I'd been sent to the mountains to write. And yet, in my mid-twenties, I was only just learning how to read in a sustainable, consistently engaged way thanks to that local store.

"YOU NEED DIVERSITY in a team, despite the conflicts it can cause, despite one's desire to be with like-minded colleagues," career bookseller Martin Latham writes in his memoir and historical miscellany *The Bookseller's Tale*. The staff of Book City in Toronto's Bloor West Village was constructed with this formula in mind. One of my colleagues, the elder of our group, used to run his own sci-fi bookshop downtown, Bakka Phoenix, named for "the weeper who mourns for all mankind" in *Dune's* Fremen legend. Another of my colleagues was a practising Buddhist and student of eccentric doom metal. There was a militant animal rights activist who split her time between the store and her local shelter. There was the friend who got me the job, a poet himself, then editor of the poetry imprint of (the now sleeping forever) Insomniac Press. There was a brilliant lyric poet, philosopher and lindy hop dancer, and the person with whom I'd have a child and buy a tree-filled property in Fredericton some ten years later.

Each evening I'd be paired with one of my colleagues. Because the evenings were slow, we would often speak to one another at length about our interests, passion projects, side hustles. To borrow a quote from Thoreau, "an infinite and unaccountable friendliness all at once like an atmosphere sustaining me" began to emerge. My colleagues and I talked—not, as I would with my fellow bellhops, about the misdeeds, attitudes and strange requests of our ultra-rich clientele, but about the books we were reading, and about the odd angles from which the bookstore allowed us to approach other, often more nebulous goals. A bookstore, but a kind of workshop too. While I've looked for and found such magic in places like concert halls, poetry readings, galleries—it has never been as clearly laid out for me as it was at Book City Bloor West Village.

One of the main organizers of this atmosphere was a budding crafter named Kalpna Patel. She was in charge of the window displays, and seemed to have a knack for grouping books together in ways that were enticing both visually and thematically, often in unexpected ways. In the years to come (and later at Type Books on Queen Street, whose managers had the good sense to give her unlimited creative freedom), she would become a bona fide book industry celebrity for this very activity. There was a Type Books window she designed that looked like the watery world of Grenadier Pond in High Park, which she filled with handmade cardboard swan sculptures. There was a window that mimicked the neon circus-tent facade of the old Honest Ed's landmark megastore, an enlarged copy of Dan Buller's cover illustration for Jesse Brown's *The Canadaland Guide to Canada* (a hilarious embrace between a moose and Toronto musician Drake) placed at the centre and framed with cheap fluorescent bulbs. There was a window display with floating jellyfish made of delicately curled paper, each curl meant to signify the attempted banning of a book.

All of these windows were gawked at on street level and, because most everyone had a camera in their pockets by then, they began to be shared widely online. The windows worked for all of the reasons important to the retail business: they were colourful, textured, eccentric and artful displays of goods. But they also magnified the interior life of a voracious reader—most of Kalpna's windows were clearly seeded from the love of a single text, phrase or idea.

Magazines and newspapers began running regular profiles of Kalpna. Her social media following grew into that strange middle branch between citizen and influencer. She began taking gigs creating large-scale displays: one for the lobby of the Art Gallery of Ontario, one for Margaret Atwood's birthday party. This work opened up an opportunity to make detailed paper-cut illustrations for a children's book about the first female Indigenous commercial pilot, Dr. Alis Kennedy (*Alis the Aviator* by Danielle Metcalf-Chenail). Kalpna's intricate paperwork illustrations unexpectedly connected with the work of her father, who built machine parts for planes, and her mother, who did textile work. *Alis the Aviator*'s publication was, Kalpna beamed online, what finally made her more eclectic but equally demanding working life visible to them.

I watched all of this mostly at a distance, from different cities, as Sue and I moved from gig to gig, trying to make our lives as writers. Meanwhile Kalpna was making this incredible life—quite literally—by hand, in the same city where we all met and sold books together. All the while, I couldn't help noticing, Kalpna remained a bookseller, even after it was clear that she could have devoted herself full-time to more lucrative large-scale design work. On a recent visit to Toronto I met her at the new Type Books location, in the neighbourhood she grew up in and lives in to this day, the Junction. While she has no ownership stake in the new store, she's now its manager, and I'm pretty sure she willed the place into existence through her work. We wandered the gentrifying streets, had one of those wide-ranging conversations that I remembered from the old days in Bloor West Village. She had all but eliminated the window display work, which had become physically taxing and left little time to read. She was happy just selling books, making plans to once again visit the small village of Aat (in Gujarat, India), where her family still has a property and where, a number of years ago—ill and dehydrated on her last week there—she had eaten fruit in the shaded part of a courtyard and spit the seeds out into the dirt. She described receiving photos over text four months later of the young members of her extended family eating watermelons picked from vines she had spit into existence. That's what people don't talk enough about, she said. The earth there yields so much.

WHEN IT'S SLOW at the bookstore in Fredericton, I sometimes immerse myself in a little bit of tree literature. One quiet Sunday afternoon I picked up a small anthology of poems about trees that has been selling (predictably) well. There I found one by William Meredith, called "Tree Marriage," which proclaims, "This gossamer we / hold each other with, this web / of love and habit is not enough." Toward a theory of sufficiency, Meredith evokes some wedding ceremonies in Bengal and Chota Nagpur, where the betrothed are wedded to themselves as well as to "tree siblings" with their "fingers barely touching in sleep / [their] threads invisible but holding."

I've been more deliberate, since my second act as a bookseller began, in searching out books that articulate the associative thrills of the local bookstore, books by writers like the great Vivian Gornick, whose prose "shake[s] the kaleidoscope of daily experience to arrive at a composition that will help mediate the pain of intimacy, the vibrancy of public space, and the exquisite intervention of strangers" (*The Odd Woman and the City*). I'm looking for the same reverence that Suzanne Simard would attach to the importance of a diversely populated forest. It's a texture of writing as well: dense, but turning suddenly from leaf to stem to light, and creating a kind of shade in which to consider the unbearable heat of the world as it currently is. A great expression for this shade is the "grammar of animacy" that botanist Robin Wall Kimmerer talks about in *Braiding Sweetgrass*. It's there in a scene where a young poet and repentant book thief encounters a bookseller in Mexico, demanding to know what kind of writer would recommend his own books to a man on his deathbed, as in Roberto Bolaño's remarkable essay "Who Would Dare?" And it's there in an inventory taken of a room belonging to abolitionist, publisher, author and businessman David Ruggles in Graham Russell Gao Hodges' biography *David Ruggles: A Radical Black Abolitionist and the*

Underground Railroad in New York City (University of North Carolina Press, 2010):

> For self-diagnosis, there were copies of *Wilson's Anatomy*, a book on the *Elements of Physiology*, and a title on consumption (tuberculosis). For spiritual assistance, Ruggles had handy a Bible, a copy of Bunyan's *Pilgrim's Progress*, and temperance documents. Augmenting his historical acumen were Macauley's *History of England* in two volumes; a history of the Mexican War, the biography of abolitionist Abel Brown, a martyr from the Underground Railroad days in New York State; and the *Prison Life and Reflections of George Thompson*, an Illinois college student imprisoned in Missouri for helping enslaved people gain liberty. To help with writing, Ruggles kept a "Worcester Dictionary," and a book of anecdotes.

Ruggles is an extraordinary example of the kind of omnivorous reader that booksellers often are, and the sort of reader that booksellers most love to sell books to. We are found in every city and town, and we orbit the local store. David Ruggles also happens to be a pivotal and overlooked figure in North American history. He was the first Black man in the United States to publish his own magazine, *The Mirror of Liberty*, which mixed poems, essays and vigilance committee meeting minutes with reports about the illegal activities of slave traders trying to recapture freed men and women. He traversed towns across the States on behalf of the publication, networking with some of the most important figures of the abolitionist movement. He helped form the New York Committee of Vigilance, which did both the intellectual and physical work of ensuring the freedom of hundreds of Black Americans. His house was a way station of the Underground Railroad. He'd head down to boats in New York Harbor and literally kick down the doors of men who were holding people against their will.

I encountered David Ruggles as my interest in the literature of booksellers intersected with the influx of books ordered into the store in support of Black Lives Matter, the Black-led movement against anti-Black racism (founded in 2013) that went worldwide in response to the 2020 murder of American George Floyd at the hands of white police officers. As the books came in, I started to do some research about Black-owned bookstores in North America. Ruggles was the first Black man in America to run his own bookstore, albeit briefly, at 67 Lispenard Street in New York City. Anti-abolitionists burned down the store, just as they'd done to his grocery store a few years earlier—one of the first grocery stores to announce it would sell food produced without the use of slave labour. Ruggles' bookstore was also a reading room and a lending library. According to Hodges' biography, Ruggles would display in the window any book that took up the abolitionist cause, regardless of whether he agreed with its contents (his biggest points of contention being with abolitionists who did not see the necessity for a more insistent and immediately physical form of activism). The immediacy resulted in a lot of fist-to-fist battles, and these took their toll. In terrible health by his early thirties, Ruggles left the city to start his own hydrotherapy clinic. He died at the age of thirty-five, surrounded by the books listed above.

PROTOCOL

The fear of God put a kind of barrier between her and the other tree planters on Pastor Jonathan's team. These were "the good guys" of supposed "good stock," the sort who didn't complain in the mess tent over breakfast about the ways the work—monotonous, repetitive, requiring every muscle in the body—invariably invaded one's dreams, nights playing out the same way as the days: three steps, spade in, handle out, seedling, handle in, foot stomp, three steps, next. She figured these dreams might put a barrier between them and whatever thoughts, illicit, violent, made them fearful. The work itself would also take on a kind of spiritual component—communion, renewal of the garden—and this seemed like enough to keep the whole team pleasant and motivated through the three long summer months.

She wasn't what you'd call the God-fearing sort herself, but her father and mother were. They'd insisted that, if she planned on planting trees again, it wouldn't be with the same group of hippies she'd hitched her wagon to last summer; they'd talk to Pastor J. Her father in particular liked to mix these anachronisms when they spoke to her: *hippie, hitched her wagon to.* She believed it was on purpose, a way of levelling the distinctions that mark specific periods within a sense of time immemorial—a sense specific only to people like her parents, what her father called their "flock."

The bits of downtime between planting that summer were filled with inane pleasantries. Offers to help light the fire or tie the laundry line when help wasn't needed. There were no wild parties. There was no Chelsea, who after her introductory handshake, took three steps backwards, dropped her drawers and pissed in the dirt. There was no Chad, with his Neil Diamond singalong drives and off-day cocaine odysseys. There was no huggy-bear Jake or fire-spinner Heather. Of course there were still singalongs and campfires, but the chords sounded cleaner and more consistent, the fire was always right where it should be, surrounded by sturdy rocks, and eight to ten metres away from the nearest tree. By the time the hymn books came out, if they came out at all, she would be asleep in her tent with her only friend from last year, the pet she'd inherited: Blair's old wolf-husky cross named Dino, whose nostrils emitted a warm little bird whistle while he slept.

She sat in the back of the Chevy Suburban at 5:30 a.m. departure. Dino was in the seat beside her, already awake and alert. This part felt more or less the same as last summer: the logging roads testing the truck's suspension. The crackling radio calls from logging trucks making sharp turns on the single lanes ahead. Spit from the mouth of her coffee cup warming the backs of her hands. There was a kind of military aspect to each morning drive, which appealed to her, just as it must have appealed to the men and boys who sat in front of her, many of whom were already in, or destined for, some kind of combat or service. Then there was the indignation she felt about the clear-cuts themselves, a common bond she shared with most every planter she'd met. One didn't have to drive too far off the tourist highways between towns to see that nature figured in this province as a kind of theatre. The backstage of every mountain was as bald as the pastor, the wildlife forced to hang their costumes up and die, the uprooted stumps like haphazard piles of wires. It made her blood boil, and it was this very rage that brought her body to life in the tent. Yes, symbiosis with nature was the hallmark of some days, but only just after the packed lunch, when she'd hit her stride. It was rage that carried her through each morning: rage at the rape of the earth, rage at the murder of her friend Blair and rage at the exorbitant amount of money she needed to earn that summer simply to continue her bachelor's degree.

Dino was different this summer too, as he must be, she thought, processing trauma in whatever way dogs do. Every summer he assumed the role of group caretaker. Dino would spend the day visiting each member of the seven-member planting team, no matter the great distances between them, the same distances that Chad, inspecting their work, had to drive. Dino would appear suddenly; she'd look with a start from the ground, seeing him trotting toward her for a scratch behind the ears. Then he'd pick a nearby stump to stand his forelegs on, make a quick captain's survey of the area, and not for the quality of seedlings she was planting but for her safety from whatever might come from the treeline, whatever might be sizing up the humans in his pack for being the enemies to nature that humans here were—forestry's scale of destruction always outweighing the small teams of bite-covered gardeners, servants to God.

Good boy, she'd tell Dino. Good boy.

This summer Dino still appeared from time to time each day to check up on her. However, as she'd confirm with her new team of planters on the truck rides home, this summer Dino made no visits to the others. And there were times Dino appeared before her looking bedraggled: burr-ridden, head low, dirt covering his nose. Only after a few weeks did it occur to her that Dino was probably out scouring the forests for Blair.

Her parents wondered why she had to be such a bleeding heart, take on the expense and the work of such a big dog. But her parents hadn't been there that night off in Prince George. They hadn't encountered the creep who'd grabbed her waist. They hadn't seen Blair grab that man's arm, then the arms of the man's three friends, or witnessed the feverish dance that ensued until the blade of someone's knife went into Blair's abdomen. They hadn't realized at four a.m., weeping in front of the hospital, that Dino was still in the parking lot back downtown. They hadn't raced on their two legs and unlocked the door of the truck and seen the desperate, hopeful look she projected into the good boy's eyes.

There was a barrier between her and the others this year, and in truth it made her work a lot easier. The ground was soft for two of the three big contracts, and she was making enough money for tuition, probably wouldn't have to go looking for work again to cover her living expenses until February, maybe March.

There were parts of this work she absolutely loved, even if she was still grieving Blair. One was the opening week's training. These workshops were mostly for newcomers, but those who'd returned from the summer before were also made to attend. In particular, she loved revisiting the protocol for encountering bears. Not those around whom you were told to lie very still and play dead, but the kinds of bears who were going to attack you regardless of whether you were already dead. With these bears you were supposed to stand on the biggest stump you could find, make yourself look huge, raise your shovel up high in the air. If the bear charged you were supposed to strike it, on the ridge of its nose, as it lunged. Both summers she had found these instructions hilarious; this idea that, in a moment of abject terror, you'd have the wherewithal to meet the menacing creature with an equal menace, to strike the bear's nose at the exact right place at the exact right moment.

Now, on a truck ride home, her thoughts turned back to pity for Dino. In a rare summer flourish of imagination, she wondered what kind of form she'd assume if Dino actually found Blair, if she were to look up in time to see them racing together toward her from the treeline. What would she do with her inevitable shock? What kind of pose would she make? Would she run toward them? Run away? Or would some kind of invisible barrier remain between them, unspoken but understood, that would force them to stop and turn back from her after a brief, distant moment of acknowledgement, and continue to forage through the remains of these ever-receding woods?

> *Our project was as medieval and as mystical as you could hope for: create a puppet show. Of all the absurdities in the world, making a puppet show seemed the most beautiful to us. Puppetry is a humble vocation[,] but one that is nonetheless ancient and profound. Its profundity rests in its humility: submission to the wood, to the form of things, the shape of a face, the smell of turpentine, the sawdust, the strange little souls that somehow glimmer in a nose or an eyebrow under your chisel… There's religion in a puppet. There [are] first principles, in a way. There [are] sorrows and joys… wind that blows between us and the world. It's all there to see if you want.*
> —The Old Trout Puppet Workshop, *Alberta Views*, July/August 2003

The following profile depicts the Old Trout Puppet Workshop as it was (and they were) in 2015–2016, while I had the chance to spend time with them at their studio and at the Blackfoot Truckstop Diner in Calgary, and to research their shows and workshops at the Banff Centre library. Since then, new shows have been produced, projects have been expanded, the studio location has changed, etc. To paraphrase a line from the essayist Elizabeth Hardwick, it's hard to hold a live trout in one's hand.

City Trout

Located in an industrial area in the Southeast quadrant of Calgary, Alberta, the original members of the Old Trout Puppet Workshop share a studio that they affectionately refer to as Fort Trout. Businesses surrounding Fort Trout include Flesher Marble & Tile, Mars Blinds & Shutters, a Sherwin-Williams Commercial Paint Store, First Place Auto, CARSTAR Chinook and their closest neighbours, with whom they share a gravel parking lot, Lucky Granite Ltd.

A white building with the hand-painted Old Trout Puppet Work-shop sign is surrounded by a half-dozen large orange shipping containers and a couple of old RVs. The containers store most of the sets and puppets from previous and currently touring shows. A garage door opens onto the front section of the studio, where the saw work and other heavy construction involved with the creation of puppet shows is done.

The rest of the interior works as a hybrid collaboration and storage space. There are a couple of large work tables. There is space to construct or operate larger puppets or set pieces. There are metal shelving units containing a disorganized mix of various puppets, puppet parts and props—severed heads, ocean backdrops, prosthetic arms, legs and genitalia. There is a beautiful dark wooden storage cabinet that the Trouts hope will one day lead a double life as a stage piece.

Judd Palmer, Pete Balkwill and Steve "Pityu" Kenderes are, for their part in the setting, the kind of bearded, rough-around-the-edges guys who have never looked out of place in an industrial stretch by the railroad tracks. But they are also winners of the Lieutenant Governor of Alberta Distinguished Artist Award, noted craftspeople of an arcane niche. And Fort Trout is a place where the province of Alberta is both built and maintained, insomuch as you believe the arts to be as essential as paved roads or curtain rods.

Fort Trout is certainly a more functional space than Pityu's first home in Calgary, an early, unofficial Trout studio, and more habitable than a previous incarnation of the studio, set in the Hudson's Bay warehouse, where dust would fall from the rafters as they hammered away at their craft.

And it is not the dream commune they once envisioned on an early version of their website ("apprentices will be slumbering in hammocks in the rafters, cooks will be chopping beautiful vegetables... people will be drawing and carving and pondering..."), an idealized, larger scale version of the place where they first gathered together at a farm in the

Alberta foothills, where they named themselves after a "legendary fish that lived at the bottom of a beloved swimming hole" and decided to pursue puppetry as a full-time vocation.

It has been almost twenty years since these multi-talented, ambitious, hard-partying magpies gathered together as friends disheartened with the directions their individual lives appeared to be taking: the colder realities of what is sometimes bullyingly and vaguely referred to as "adulthood." Having experimented with puppet theatre for a number of years, they at least saw clearly that it was puppetry that gave them a sense of joy and purpose. And in the foothills of Alberta they decided they wanted that joy and purpose to be central to their lives.

Performing Trout

Since 1999, Calgary's Old Trout Puppet Workshop has toured across Canada and internationally with a series of unique shows that push the limits of what a puppet is and what a puppet is capable of communicating.

They are two decades in as an official entity, have produced ten full shows: *The Unlikely Birth of Istvan, The Tooth Fairy, Beowulf, The Last Supper of Antonin Carême, Pinnocchio, Famous Puppet Death Scenes* (probably their most well-known work), *The Erotic Anguish of Don Juan, Ignorance, Jabberwocky* and *Ghost Opera.*

They have industrial packing crates' worth of side projects as well. They have produced a short Christmas film, *From Naughty to Nice*, in collaboration with the National Film Board. Their work was featured in a 2008 music video for Feist's "Honey Honey." They designed the set for the National Arts Centre's recent production of *Twelfth Night* and the Vancouver Opera's production of *Hansel and Gretel*. They collaborate on theatre productions with Western Canadian companies such as Victoria's Puente Theatre Society, as well as Trout-inspired outfits like Toronto's Clunk Puppet Lab. The Agnostic Mountain Gospel Choir is a Tom Waits–inspired howling band that counts both Judd and Pete as members. Judd's written a series of children's books, three of which have been nominated for the Governor General's Award. Pete and Bob Davis (the Trouts' general manager) curate the International Festival of Animated Objects, an organization with which the company has had a long relationship as participants.

Under the umbrella of the Canadian Academy of Mask and Puppetry (CAMP), Pete has an extensive teaching career at institutions such as the University of Calgary and the Banff Centre; he also offers individual workshops in Calgary and around the world. Pityu is a practising painter and sculptor. Add to all of this their dreams—both as a collective and as individuals—for future Old Trout presences in film, television, a large artistic commune in the woods. The crates fill up.

Technical Trout

The Old Trouts' trademark puppet is one that requires the puppeteer to insert their head into the puppet's empty torso. The puppeteer peers out the puppet's stomach, chest or neck. The puppeteer's hands connect near the wrists of the puppet, allowing a full range of motion with the puppet's arms.

"They sit upon the head and come instantly alive," says Pete, "and are capable of many things. Both arms are free to work." The puppet's legs, if it has legs, will sometimes rest decoratively on the puppeteer's shoulders. But it's the puppeteer's own bounding and leaping, sometimes from behind a barrier, more often out in full view of the audience, that becomes the central means by which the puppet moves around the stage.

Back inside the puppet's rib cage, the mechanics are such that when the puppeteer turns their head, the puppet's head will turn. This kind of technology, Pityu explains, is quite typical of head puppets. One signature structural contribution the Trouts have made to this style of puppet is a chinstrap enabling the puppeteer's own mouth movements to dictate the mouth movements of the puppet. The same rods affixed to the chinstrap will often attach to the eyebrows of the puppet as well as to the mouth, lending an added layer of expression.

Sometimes the puppeteer's own voice, speaking from within the puppet's chest, will act as the voice of the puppet. Often, as in their version of *Pinocchio*, the puppet will communicate in an unintelligible gibberish, in howls, cries and whimpers—in exaggerated tones rather than articulated speech. This kind of communication works well in dialogue with an actor on stage, such as in *Don Juan*, or in tandem with an omniscient narrator, such as the one employed in *Ignorance*. In such configurations, the otherness of the puppet is highlighted through nonsense, and the function of these actors and narrators will (at least in part) become that of the puppet's translator.

As Pityu walks me through the shop and introduces me to some of the puppets, he talks about the difference in materials, from lightweight polystyrene to the more traditional wood. "Wood has become more prohibitive as the shows get larger," he says. "There's more weight. It's harder to travel." The Trouts' Pinocchio puppet is laid out on a metal table. Pityu picks the puppet up and places it over his head, in order to best illustrate the head puppet's full range of motion.

The collective's aim is to be "at the service of the puppet," and the design of these head puppets provides ample opportunity for the puppeteers to humble themselves before their masters. The puppeteer, in such a configuration, is essentially masked.

"Mask work really comes into it," Pete says, "and the physical application is great." The puppeteer, often clad in a pair of grey full-body underwear (the Trouts' signature costume), is meant to be no more than the mound of gravel or body of water beneath the living form. Judd would later talk about the general philosophy of their puppetry as being about such "direct physical contact—the performer connected directly to the object, without separation by strings or clever mechanisms."

As I watch Pityu, other images relating to the connection between such a puppet and its puppeteer come to mind: the puppeteer as something of the pack horse, carrying its exuberant rider wherever the story goes. The puppeteer as the father or mother with their child on their shoulders. (The child Abigail, the central character of *The Tooth Fairy*, is cleverly played by an unmasked adult woman. Her costume incorporates smaller arms, synthetic legs, and a child's dress to make her appear as part head puppet, part human).

Whatever the image conjures for an attendee of an Old Trout show, it is altogether different, as Judd has suggested, from the image of the traditional godlike puppeteer who works the marionette from above.

Orbiting Trout

The Trouts draw from an enormous range of influences across the historical tradition of puppetry. Sometimes these influences are conscious. Sometimes the similarities are happy accidents.

One of the Trouts' major (and conscious) influences is the long and rich Japanese tradition of puppetry called Bunraku, where at least three people are required to operate a single puppet. Eva, one of Don Juan's mistresses in *The Erotic Anguish of Don Juan*, is one such Bunraku-inspired puppet. Performed by the requisite three puppeteers, the parts of her body that have been highlighted by the puppet makers— arms, face, chest, legs—acquire a lithe, spectacular and comic range of motion as she performs a seductive dance onstage. One puppeteer is charged with her head and the left arm, another with her right arm (the arm with which she eventually pins Don Juan to the ground). The third puppeteer acts as Eva's legs and chest. Eva's breasts are affixed to this puppeteer's forehead. Eva's legs, more or less an elaborately healed pair of crutches, are controlled by the puppeteer's arms.

There is a deliberately cultivated demeanour of intense concern to the puppeteers: as Pityu explains, their own focus is meant to draw the attention away from the puppeteer and toward the puppets themselves. But it's easy to see that this demeanour is also in the service of a kind of comedy through contrasts, their seriousness played for laughs against the oftentimes outsized or exaggerated emotional life of the puppet.

The Old Trout aesthetic also has roots in the puppet theatre of Prague and the rest of the Czech Republic. Early on, Judd travelled to the Czech Republic with then collaborator Xstine Cook—one of the founders of Alberta's Green Fools Theatre Society—for the specific purpose of immersing themselves in the country's puppet theatre (a tradition that goes back to the Middle Ages).

There have been group research trips to Mexico, a country that also has a vibrant history of puppet theatre. There have been tours through a number of parts of Western and Eastern Europe, and many of these tours have included a research element.

The Trouts have a healthy respect for the contemporary puppet theatre community. Prominent puppet theatre companies in the Western Hemisphere include Portugal's Marionetas do Porto, as well as the politically active Bread and Puppet Theatre that emerged in New York as part of an anti-war movement and is now based in Vermont. The most famous puppet theatre company in the world right now is probably South Africa's Handspring, which has been producing and touring internationally for thirty years, and employs a full-time staff of twenty in their puppet factory in Cape Town.

War Horse, an adaptation of a novel by Michael Morpurgo put on by Britain's National Theatre, features Handspring's extraordinarily lifelike, three-puppeteer-operated horse puppets. These puppets use nostril and ear movements to make the horses come even more alive. Joey, the protagonist's horse, might be the most famous individual puppet in the live-theatre world right now (though Elmo and other television puppets will, like famous movie actors, always outshine their live-theatre counterparts in terms of fame, fortune and notoriety).

Pete, waxing admiringly of the technical invention of the Handspring horse, stressed that the Old Trouts are, to a point, still devotees of a certain small-scale, on-the-farm aesthetic. In plays such as the *Tooth Fairy*, and most certainly *The Erotic Anguish of Don Juan*, there has been an attempt to explore large-scale puppets. Yet Pete expressed concern that puppetry that tries for too grand a scale, like some of the puppets popularized in plays such as *War Horse*, risk betraying the potential intimacy of the puppet-audience experience. The puppets in these kinds of experiments often "run the risk of turning into stage props."

Pondering Trout

What makes for a successful puppet, a puppet that is more than mere stage prop? Because the Old Trouts are three separate individuals with three strong personalities, a consensus on what the company's ideal kind of puppet *is* will always, like the nature of their performances, be somewhat open to change and evolution. Pete stresses the "fallibility" and "intimacy" of the puppets. A successful puppet, for him, fully inhabits a certain expression and sense of character: "There are certain puppets that you care about instantly... They seem alive the minute someone touches them."

As a professionally trained actor whose research interests and expertise include the Tadashi Suzuki technique and other applications concerned with the actor's bodily presence, Pete is perhaps the most concerned with the puppet's breath, its manipulation, its focus, its fixed point—"the four key points you want to hit when animating a puppet," according to a short video promoting his Puppetry Intensive at the Banff Centre. This concern for the bodily presence of the puppet plays a role right from the point of construction, where Pete is, according to his cohorts, the most likely to obsess over the making of a particular puppet, to toil over getting the intended expression of the puppet just right.

Judd speaks to the potential the puppet has to shift emotions, to do drastic and surprising things. He describes the successful puppet, for him, as having "a certain kind of wistfulness, an unspoken sorrow of some kind, expressed in the tilt of an eyebrow or the edge of the mouth, something that makes us feel a softness towards it."

Expanding on Pete's idea of fallibility, Judd goes on to describe a successful puppet as also communicating an unease or unpredictability, one rooted in its specific character traits, but also in the idea, he says, that "on some ancient, fundamental level, a puppet is a monster. Not, like, a dragon or griffin or something grand; a hobgoblin, maybe—but monstrous nonetheless."

"My favourite puppets," Judd says, "have that quality of having a secret."

Pityu applies the paint to all of the puppets when they are finished, and is often, according to him, the one who "somehow ends up making the first puppet for every new show." Pityu sees the successful puppet as being able to "shrink scale" and "change time." Like Pete, he is enamoured by the idea of the puppet as a tool for eliciting empathy. He also sees some of the unforeseen attributes that the puppets acquire during their making, the kinds of secrets that Judd talks about, as playing an essential role in the overall feel and action of the play. These unforeseen attributes, he says, will "often change the direction of the entire performance." And this ability to change the direction of the performance is another kind of agency the puppets will acquire during the creation of an Old Trout play.

Pete's emotional connection with the puppets is evident whenever he appears on stage. Watch him act as the shaking hand of a despairing puppet in *Ignorance*, a puppet who crawls out to his window ledge and makes the frightening leap. And to watch Judd manipulate and narrate through Tweak, the connective tissue of *Famous Puppet Death Scenes*, is to experience the absolute glee of allowing a piece of carved wood to wax passionately on life's brief and beautiful fires.

Pityu, who feels that as an actor on stage he shares a puppet's "tendency to mug," is probably the Trout who looks the most like a mountain man. As such, he is often employed (quite happily) as a kind of extension or important aspect of a particular puppet, the one whose own burly, bug-eyed physical characteristics make him best suited to enter the material orbit of the objects on stage.

Playing the devil in *The Erotic Anguish of Don Juan*, Pityu was clad in in a fur hat and accessories, riding a tricycle with a giant, snorting bull's head affixed to the handlebars. Judd describes how, in their earliest feature as an official collective, *The Unlikely Birth of Istvan*, the company had Pityu, between a pair of wooden legs, "literally birthed onto the stage."

Mortal Trout

All three men agree the Trouts' ideas about puppetry reached collaborative unity in 2006's *Famous Puppet Death Scenes* (FPDS). The show comprises a sequence of short scenes from made-up "famous puppet plays." In each scene a different puppet meets its untimely demise.

The jumping-off point for this play was a scene in their version of *Pinocchio*, which drew from the pre-Disneyfied, original 1883 script by the Italian writer Carlo Collodi. A scene from this version had Pinocchio bash a cricket to death with a hammer, and the Trouts played this scene up with a gory glee. While all three of the puppeteers had mentioned this particular scene and its influence on the creation of FPDS to me separately, there's an article by Celia Wren, for the publication *American Theatre*, which contains the most illustrative quote (from Judd) about how the audience reaction to this particular scene in *Pinocchio* gave the Trouts their idea for a full-length play focusing specifically on puppet deaths: "At first they were shocked," Judd recalls. "There was an intake of breath; and they laughed; and then it actually started to seem terribly sad; and then tragic; and then this great existential hole opened in the theatre, and everybody fell through it and came out the other end feeling happy!"

The quick-cut format of FPDS, on the heels of the more drawn-out narratives of *Pinocchio* and *Beowulf*, brought back, according to Pete, a lot of the sense of spontaneity and collaboration of the company's original endeavours. Many more than three puppeteers worked on FPDS, and Pete, Judd and Pityu all agree that the ease with which individuals were able to invest in particular scenes and in individual ideas created a bedrock where everyone felt integral to the play's creation. That it was a collective joy to stitch these various macabre, faux-famous performances together.

The opening sequence of FPDS, taken from the "renowned" play *The Feverish Heart* by Nordo Frot, opens with dramatic opera music. A bald hand puppet in a pale-grey suit enters the stage, observes the audience just as a large fist appears over his head. The fist crushes his balloon-like skull mere seconds later. With that initial audience shock and belly laugh out of the way, the narrator of FPDS, a half-naked, grey-haired old puppet named Tweak, gives us "a moment to recover" before "yanking the mortal strings."

For the next hour the troupe mixes punchline comedy with true horror and sadness, each puppet fulfilling its duty to die with unique tonal *and* technical attributes, the combination giving the audience not just a broad sampling of mortal ends, but also a broad sampling of the possible ways a puppet might be alive to the audience.

In *The Cruel Sea* by Thorvik Skarsbarg (Hour 14), the curtain opens to a mustachioed puppet, looking part postal worker, part soldier. He is stone still inside a wallpapered room. There is a broken window, a dusting of snow on the sill. Then a hand appears through the broken glass. It is alive for a second, only to rest on the sill for the remainder of the scene, a hint that some kind of massacre has occurred outside. For a while the only thing moving is an old woman in a shawl, who appears a few times in the window over the course of the two-minute scene. It's as if she's just going about her day outside, trying to ignore whatever horrors have recently occurred. Meanwhile, the man indoors remains fixed where he is. We can see thin sticks protruding from various points on his head, face, arms and torso. As time stretches on, and the room grows darker, and the woman continues to circle the perimeter, the sticks begin to pull sections of the man away from his face and body— first the skin off his ear, then the skin off his cheek, then a section of his hat… He is already dead, and what we are seeing is the process of decomposing, from painted figure to, by the end of the scene, a far less detailed but still visibly human block of wood. The old woman continues to circle. Curtain. No laughter, but much applause.

Darker still, the next puppet death scene features an oversized book wheeled out on a cart. The puppeteer is Judd, silent and serious in his funeral suit. The title of the book Judd displays before the audience is *Never Say It Again* by L.M. Snuck. Tipped onto its side, the book is unlocked and shown to contain, as its pages, a number of large canvases. Each canvas depicts a farmhouse from a distance. Each turning page brings us a closer view of the house. Judd occasionally leans in to hear what we soon learn (though already sense) to be screams. But Judd shuts the book and wheels it away before we get right up to the door.

Collaborative Trout

The Trouts all collaborate on the initial ideas for their plays—what to perform, how to stage it, ways they'd like to evolve and expand their repertoires as puppeteers. Each play will evolve according to the look of the puppets and the conversations that ensue between the three during the construction of the characters and the set. As Pityu describes it, they're often "building the show at the same time they are learning their roles."

Judd is often the primary writer. When I asked him about some of the personal stories behind the plays, he enumerates broad themes based on interactive dynamics within the group. *The Unlikely Birth of Istvan* is, according to him, "an ode to our birth as a company... to disparate elements coming together." *The Last Supper of Antonin Carême* is a play where "an imbalance between us, or an uncertainty about how to collaborate arose." "We were no longer so sure," he says of the play, but also perhaps of the collective, "about how to join the different elements together." *Pinocchio* grapples with their ideas of childishness. *Ignorance*, he suggests, is "a play about middle age." Both *The Last Supper* and *Beowulf* "grapple with the idea of pride." This pride, whether manifest as individuals toward the collective, or as a collective against the business-as-usual world, has, I sensed, been tempered by time, and by the degree of success that has allowed them to survive for so many years as puppeteers.

Pete describes the "odd vibrancy" of the collective as being rooted more in their roles as friends than as puppeteers. Over the course of my conversations with all three Trouts, there were plenty of hints about times where the three had argued, held grudges or been burdened by an enormous amount of doubt. But at no time did I sense anything resembling bitterness between them. And at no time during individual talks did any of them lay any claim to having been any more central to the success of the company than the others. Yes, Pityu might be the one who often makes each play's first puppet, and in the end unifies them all in some way with his paintbrush. Yes, Pete might be the most skilled as a puppeteer and as an actor, the one who first asked more technical, practical theatre questions like, Do we have a director? Do we have a stage manager? during their initial experiments, and the one with the teaching skills best suited to spreading the gospel of Old Trout puppetry. Yes, Judd might be the one whose skills and storytelling abilities establish the narrative arc of each play, spearhead their ventures into film, and in a large way write the myth of the company as a whole. But all three of them have a profound understanding, not just of what the other men bring to the table, but of how their skills and their personalities complement one another; how the mix is, in fact, essential to their survival. All three of them spoke nostalgically about some variation of what Pete called "moments of pure collaboration"; they appear driven to continue their artistic pursuits in part with the hope that, with each new project, the possibility exists that the three of them might reunite in that alchemical place once again.

They also encourage one another's artistic interests outside of the company. Some of this comes from an understanding of the various elements of theatre, engineering and acting that go into puppetry. But it's also, more generally, a question of happiness, and of how to stay engaged with the world. During a video call from his home in Victoria, Judd says, quite succinctly, that they all know that no one art form "will bring ecstasy, salvation and a salary."

Fledgling Trout

Located in Kananaskis country, just a short drive outside of Calgary, Camp Chief Hector emphasizes community and values-based education, outdoor challenge, fun, individual growth, environmental stewardship, leadership development and service excellence
—official website for YMCA's Camp Chief Hector

"We saw ourselves as oddballs," Judd says over breakfast at the twenty-four-hour Blackfoot Truckstop Diner, a sixty-year-old Calgary time capsule near Fort Trout. "We did puppet shows for the kids [at Camp Chief Hector], too. A lot of elaborate, and—we see now—deeply offensive initiation-type rituals. But, more significantly, a number of broad, abstract stuff, like Pityu in diapers, playing a character we just called 'Humanity.'"

Judd would get a job with Parks Canada a year or so later, at an interpretive programming centre. Part of the program involved designing educational puppets and scale models. He saw an opportunity to gather Pete, Pityu and the others to work with more elaborate materials.

"We had a lot of freedom to create at the interpretive centre," Pete explained, "so it was an obvious move."

Pete is convinced that the Trouts were somehow fated to join each other. He makes a number of strong points, including the part-time job he once had as a driver for Judd's grandfather's wife. This was ten years before the Trouts had formed and a couple of years before they all met at Camp Chief Hector. It was a job that had actually brought him to the Palmer family ranch on more than one occasion.

The group maintained their friendships through the early nineties, each at various stages of completing university degrees. The group also travelled around the world a great deal as individuals. As Judd says,

"There was a certain search for enlightenment going on among the future members of the collective."

One of the experiences Judd cited as integral to the Old Trout's history was a play he put on at the University of Toronto around 1994. He'd been granted two hundred dollars by the Trinity College Dramatic Society to put on a play he'd written about the former Czech dictator Klement Gottwald and his widow, Petra. It was revealed during this conversation that a mutual friend of ours, poet and mathematician Hugh Thomas, was cast as Petra after the woman Judd had originally asked refused. I followed up with Hugh to get a non-Trout perspective on the experience: "I think he had encountered a news item about Gottwald's head having been embalmed and saved by his widow," Hugh writes in an email. "Eventually she was unable to buy food for the dog, who was driven by hunger to consume some of the embalmed head of his former master, which killed him… This became the germ of the plot, whose dramatis personae consisted of Gottwald's head, Gottwald's body, the dog, and Gottwald's wife."

Judd recalls having to pass the play off as the work of an imaginary Czech absurdist playwright called Blednu Cestovani in order to convince the Trinity College Dramatic Society that it was worth performing.

According to Judd, *Blednu Cestovani* translates to something like "to grow pale by travelling."

The show was a success, and was later picked up by a one-act-play festival in Calgary. Back on home turf, Judd collaborated on the set design for the play with Pityu. As the legend goes, they had to pass off Judd to the festival as the visiting Blednu Cestovani, replete with a fake accent.

"I felt guilty about this," says Judd, "and later travelled to the Czech Republic with Xstine Cook to learn about Czech theatre and immerse myself in its culture; mostly out of interest, but partly as a kind of penance."

The story seems too good to be true. As Pete says, "Judd will often exaggerate things in the service of myth-making." Even the story of the Old Trout that the group named themselves after, a fish who would supposedly "answer any question you ask, if you could find it," was an embellishment added as the company was gaining traction and being interviewed by various newspapers. As Judd revealed to me, it "makes a better explanation for our name than the actual explanation, which is: we can't quite remember why we chose that name." He goes on: "We thought it meant 'old friend' in Newfoundland. Apparently Newfoundlanders will call a child a trout if it does something endearing. In England Old Trout means 'old lady.'"

Whatever the exact details of the Cestovani play, it was an important bit of early creative success. It certainly made Judd question whether university dramatic societies were the best places to spread his wings as a puppeteer. More importantly, it brought Judd back to Calgary, where he and Pityu and other future Trout members began a four-year collaboration (1995–1999) with the Green Fools and other members of Calgary's alternative culture scene.

The Green Fools, as established theatre performers, were becoming increasingly interested in puppetry. They produced a number of shows of which future members of the Old Trouts were principle authors and collaborators: *The Death of Benvenuto Cellini* (the fruit of Xstine and Judd's travels to Prague, backed by a Dada music ensemble called Street of Crocodiles); *Punch and Judy*; *Bosch* (based on the *Triptych of the Temptation of St. Anthony*); *The Ice King* (a tale about the men aboard the doomed Franklin Expedition. According to Judd it was "possibly a very good play, hard to tell. The play was basically about men freezing to death, and it was debuted in the middle of a Calgary heat wave.")

The Old Trouts might have remained Green Fools, but that company's founding members were becoming more and more interested in street circus and other brands of outdoor performances, in integrating their work into the fabric of city life. Judd, Pityu and the others were quite clear that they wanted the controlled environments of indoor the-atre stages, the ability to tour, and some of them had lofty dreams of performing in large-scale theatre settings (dreams that, as it happens, have come true).

Gathering Trout

[W]ith the cold autumn wind upon them, they had decided that the future held only two directions: They were either going to open up a flea circus or commit themselves to an insane asylum… They talked about how to make little clothes for fleas by pasting pieces of colored paper on their backs… They talked about making little flea wheelbarrows and pool tables and bicycles.

They would charge fifty-cents admission for their flea circus. The business was certain to have a future in it. Perhaps they would even get on the Ed Sullivan Show.

—"Trout Fishing in America" by Richard Brautigan

Many of the original Trouts had already been gathering intermittently at the Palmer ranch throughout their youths and into their adult lives. It was, according to "Notes on the Art of Puppetry in an Atmosphere of Dread," a 2003 Trout-authored *Alberta Views* article, "an anchor when we felt storm-tossed or when our notions were growing thin, a mythic and mystical place that embodied our connection." More practically, it had also been the place where Pityu and Judd had acquired or borrowed farm equipment for Pityu's sculptures. These sculptures were large-scale, motor-driven pieces and dioramas that incorporated puppets. So the strings between the Palmer ranch and puppetry were, by the mid-nineties, already starting to move.

Judd and former Trout Stephen Pearce, in the previously mentioned *Alberta Views* article, suggest that it was the fear and panic precipitating the turn of the millennium that had driven them to the ranch to make puppet shows in 1999. Pete, who entered the fray a few months after the initial group had gotten together, describes it thus: "Judd had the magic horn and blew it."

To earn their keep, the Trouts had to do odd jobs around the farm. It's difficult to tell it any better than Judd and Stephen Pearce already have:

> We felt a strength returning to us as we toiled. In the dark mornings, the mountains cold and enormous over us, we delivered hay to horses with frost on our whiskers and clouds of steam puffing into the air from their huge warm lungs. We collected eggs, fed the pigs, damaged tractors. And then back to the [puppet] workshop, where we would work into the night, growing shaggy as the days passed.

The ranch may have also provided the opportunity for a consideration of scale. Separate from the mythic tales of artistic camaraderie, separate from the heroic template of turning away from the trappings of the modern world in order to pursue a humble vocation, separate from all of this, I think, is the image of a bunch of human beings living and working somewhere at the foot of the mountains. While farther into the Prairies the farmer may see nothing but sky for miles and miles, may understand themselves as being in direct contact with the void or with a god, I think that the landscape particular to this part of Alberta gives a different impression: the image of something bigger than oneself always being somewhere *just over there*—a major factor, whether material or spiritual, that animates a life. The conversation between mountain and human is akin to the conversation between puppeteer and puppet. One may see the enormity and potential of oneself, but also the poverty of one's own materials, one's absolute smallness.

Ambassador Trout

Pete Balkwill's Puppet Intensive at the Banff Centre is one example of the kind of branching out that all of the members of the Old Trout Puppet Workshop do in order to promote their art form, earn a living and ensure both the viability and visibility of the company. Pete is married and has children. Judd and his wife, Mercedes Bátiz-Benét, herself a respected playwright and theatre director (and frequent Trout collaborator), live with their young son in Victoria. While both Pete and Judd are still deeply in love with the craft, writing and production of puppet theatre, neither of them is very much interested in remaining, or able to remain, as touring members for a large portion of the year. Now those jobs are often given to some of the numerous actors and puppeteers eager to work with the company. Projects like the *Twelfth Night* stage design are ideal. What would be even more ideal for someone like Judd is if the film and television work continued, allowing him to move back and forth between his Victoria home and Fort Trout without any sidetracks.

Pityu is the one Trout who still tours with every production. His responsibilities at home in Halifax are less traditionally defined, so it's often easier for him to be away for long stretches. He says there are slow days at the easel in his tree-fort painting studio, days where he feels eager for Judd or Pete to call from the opposite side of the country and say a new project is on. Seventeen years later, he still loves the experience of being on the road.

There are also numerous practical benefits to an original Trout being on tour. It ensures that the sets on stage look the same as they did when first built by Judd, Pete and Pityu at Fort Trout. When a puppet or stage prop inevitably breaks, it is important that someone familiar with the initial construction is there to fix things. More broadly, Pityu says, it's important "to be a kind of ambassador for the original troupe, to ensure there is that presence."

That presence is not insignificant to maintaining the overall spirit of the company. The Trouts continue to feel that spirit as a trio, either while building at Fort Trout or on the occasions when their schedules allow them to perform together. But if Judd and Pete both tend to think more broadly and abstractly about the continuing existence, and future projects and offshoots, of the Workshop, Pityu tries to remain flexible enough to help with the practical application of these broader visions, such as set and graphic design.

Pityu sleeps in one of those old RVs out in the gravel parking lot while he's in Calgary. Judd and Pete both make a point to mention this, and seem to enjoy that a bit of the early mountain camp-out remains a part of their day-to-day workspace. When Pityu says that he wants to be "someone who tells fantastical tales in a fantastical fashion," it's a feeling that one can apply to the whole collective, to where they've been, and to what they hope to continue to do.

When I went to talk with Pityu at the studio, he pointed me toward the kitchen where, with no running water in the RV, he had been forced to fashion a homemade shower system that connected with a water pipe inside Fort Trout. He had acquired an inflatable kiddie pool, which he had to place upon a table so that the hose could connect to the water source above him. A circular rod and shower curtain had also been affixed to the rafters.

The shower was an outlandish, but totally functional, contraption. There amid the skulls and shrunken masks, the leather breasts and heads of bulls, it brought to mind the image of a pond, something not unlike the swimming hole at the Palmer ranch—a kind of timeless, troutful thing that the Stoney-Nakoda, farmers, cowboys or hikers would gather around: maybe to bathe, maybe to fish, maybe to write a poem or to carve a walking stick, or maybe, as the audience to some elemental theatre, to just sit and watch the lights play over the water.

THE APARTMENT ABOVE THE SHOP

Cellists were our upstairs neighbours

practising
intermittently
every day

When they moved
they moved
on the animal skins
of their feet

When they vacated
to somewhere across the park

with their suitcases
and their shell cases

we cried
as the stomps
of new tenants
rained paint chips
onto the shelves

into the ears
of our winter boots

Cellists were our upstairs neighbours

To keep thinking of them
is to lay strings
over a hole
in the roof

FRESHET AND LONG CROSS

Carl had gotten the idea for the all-wheel park during a lunch-break trip to the public library. In the old days you might have called what they were living in "the year of the flood," but the reality was the floods were now happening every year. Meltwater from the north was heading downriver each spring at greater and greater speeds, with less and less riverside forest floor slowing the roll. Each year folks were hauling sopping-wet furniture up from their basements, appliances rendered useless; each year some poor farmer's chickens would turn up bobbing near another farm seven kilometres away, half of them already dead and upside down.

He'd gotten the idea at the library, looking out to a parking lot where no cars were currently able to park. Parking meters poked out of the water. Water lapped right up to the library's bricks. It would have been an apocalyptic scene if not for three kids who, safety advisories be damned, rode their BMX bikes from the walking bridge ramp and into the shin-high water, tires leaving wakes on the brown-green surface.

Carl worked for the City of Freshet as one of the civil engineers charged with developing and overseeing public projects in concert with business developments, and everything in his working life moved slower than he would like. The future city of Freshet that Carl imagined was in a physically different location from where Freshet currently was, uphill on both the north and south sides. But to transport an entire downtown a few hundred metres up the embankments was not just a matter of moving concrete. It was about moving the very idea of the city in the minds of the citizens—theirs, and the minds of the generations before them, which the living still carried. This undertaking, as he was learning, would require at least as many psychologists and cultural historians as it would engineers, demolition teams, welders and electricians. He knew this because the developers of new hotels and apartment buildings were still opening their wallets to the waterfront. Even a brand new riverside opera house, with a price tag of 360 million dollars, was in the final stages of planning.

Carl spent most of his meetings with these developers quietly fuming to himself, and not without notice from Sarah, his boss. Carl had known Sarah all his life, gone to school with her, eaten barbecue with her, been invited to the gallery openings and powwows that her family was always integral to organizing. Her family lived on the neighbouring community of Long Cross—mother, father and brothers the latest iterations of a long line of canoe makers, stretching back to long before the arrival of the Europeans. Her family was passionately, and sometimes lucratively, keeping the tradition alive: sealing cedar-bark hulls with pine resin and bear grease, refurbishing canoes reclaimed from the dusty attics of colonialism—the oldest of which was to be the centrepiece of the new opera house lobby. While her two brothers had taken to the family trade, Sarah had, some time between her second and third year of university, become convinced that the only way to make sure the devil had a room for you in the house was to be there when the blueprints were drawn. As she continued her upward trajectory in government, her urgencies and commitments shifted; she knew that her relational ideas of architecture and land were both more nuanced and more practical than those of the colonizers who held the deeds and signed the cheques. Someone who could have worked anywhere in the world, she chose to remain at home, in one of the few places where the idea of a reasonably peaceful, coterminous existence with the settlers sometimes seemed plausible. Even the new opera house, the supposed "crown jewel" (loaded settler term) would have a facade engraved with traditional fiddleheads, and 33 percent of the feature operas would be written in the traditional language of her ancestors. These were the kinds of stipulations she was usually steadfast about. At her best, she wove her ideals and her consciousness of the historical and ongoing genocide of her people through the hard consonants of settler capitalism with expert skill, making things better for her people and by extension, the settler citizens in her orbit. At her worst, life in meeting rooms with the outsized expectations of both communities wore her down—made her feel like some kind of heavy hybrid, she sometimes confided to Carl, drowning under the weight of racist, divisive and dangerous realities that could not, no matter her efforts, be made less real.

Sarah brought Carl into his office and told him, "There's already too much parking riverside. Think of something useful we can build that might assuage your fears somewhat, real as they are. Something that won't be totally destroyed or rendered useless by the freshets, but that wouldn't have us abandoning the riverside entirely. It's where people have been and want to be, to work and play, in spite of what happens, and in spite of your fear. Make it good, Carl. I can't have you here every meeting with your judgy pouts, potentially sandbagging thousands of contracts and jobs. I love you, but for the past few years, you've been making this harder for me than it already is. You know this is already too damn hard."

~&

Carl had been racking his brain for weeks. Not another playground, another concert stage. He thought about something more pointedly cynical, and often shared these ideas with his family over dinner: a boathouse called Futures, or even a series of exaggeratedly large aquariums with open tops to strain the sofas, road signs and plastic jugs of detergent from the floods, creating a yearly display of conceptual art and civic inventory.

Here at the library, as he got up to move closer to the window, Carl almost forgot his two mystery novels and the copy of *A Pattern Language* he checked out every few months simply to ensure it remained in circulation. He watched a kid pop up on one wheel of his bike and turn twice in the water before lowering the other wheel down. He watched their utter disregard for blue-green toxic algae and other dangerous bacteria from the farms, mills and factories upriver. Unlike the disregard of real estate developers—who knew better, who were already changing the fine print of their insurance policies—this brand of ignorance Carl could revel in, the fluid ways they moved, untethered, perhaps, by any foundational knowledge, its mortar of paranoia. Carl checked out his books, made sure his pant legs were properly tucked into his wellingtons, ran out the door and gave each of the kids a copy of his business card. He told them that, with permission from their parents, he wanted them at City Hall for some brainstorming sessions. He went back to his office, out of breath, sat down in front of his drafting board and began to draw.

~&

The planning sessions were some of the most extraordinary times Carl can remember in his working life. He encouraged the kids to imagine the wildest possibilities, which they would winnow down to something within the 1.5-million-dollar budget. They were reluctant to contribute at first, but his willingness to sit in long silence, to hold an eager, open gaze, eventually wore their suspicions down, convinced them their input could be potentially limitless, and was of value.

On the second meeting the dams broke. Bowls of various depths and undulations would be required. Extended, grindable surfaces. They sourced the smoothest, most forgiving kinds of materials. They tried, together, to anticipate the flow and flights of in-line skaters and stunt bikers the way meteorologists must anticipate the movements of clouds. The days would end with crushed juice boxes and dented pop cans littered over the conference table, and Carl would have a sketchbook full of coral, of viruses hatched from the labs of comic book scientists. The final iteration of the park was all surfaces; there would be nothing within the structure that the weather could destroy, that would need to be reclaimed or repaired. If anything the bowls of the all-wheel park would cup the water in the ways of those cynical aquarium tanks he once pictured. The water would eventually recede, and the children would return, stinking of marijuana and dirty socks, each with a recording device in their pockets, testing each other's limits, the heights they could fly to, their thresholds for pain, and setting these rides to the kinds of music Carl would try to bob his head to even if he couldn't understand the lyrics, even if the beat made his brain feel like someone had set it on fire.

~&~

A year later, on a slightly overcast day in March, Carl, Sarah, the kids and a few hundred others watched the mayor cut the ribbon on the Freshet all-wheel park. For the first couple of weeks, everything worked as it was supposed to, a palpable vibrancy building downtown with each passing day. Coffee shops reported increased business. The library had a few more stragglers, even if it was mostly kids looking for somewhere to pee. Sarah gave Carl a little fist pump whenever he walked by her office. Most everyone in the city agreed on the park's aesthetic merit; a writer at the local newspaper even likened it to a prom-night carnation, pinned to the river's lapel.

A few weeks later, Carl was swirling the dishes in the suds of the kitchen sink, thinking about his own hobbies and passion projects, which he had been neglecting for way too long. That night he opened the dictionary of the traditional language of the people of Long Cross.

This hobby had roots in a general desire to assuage his white settler guilt over genocide and land theft, no doubt. But there were other reasons. As he was more and more in consultation on projects with people from the reserve, sometimes a well-placed *hello* in the traditional language went a long way toward paving a road.

And there was a playful part of his interest, too, that had something to do with language's relationship to architecture. He was fascinated with how this language removed English's glittering excess of adjectives and rooted an individual both structurally and organizationally in the world immediately around them, from a lexicon made of the place where he was right now.

Finally, a lot of his learning also had to do with Sarah, whom he'd been trying to impress all his life. But Sarah was never enthusiastic about his bumbling attempts, in her family's language, at *Thanks*, or *How's your son?* One night at a local bar called the Gondola, after a particularly rough week of negotiations, she had accused Carl of not really admiring her culture at all. Sarah said what he admired was simply her own exceptionalism, the racist implication of difference from her own people which she said, was a white, neoliberal kind of sickness, one that made influencing and life coaching into careers, picking only the most obviously appealing flowers from a soil that was still being poisoned by the dominant culture to which he belonged. Of course she'd been infected, through a myopically Eurocentric education, with these same ideas, she said while pressing her finger too hard into her collarbone. She had hoped her own abilities to navigate the settler's world, to lobby for her people, would endear her somehow to her parents. But after many years she was starting to realize that whatever she did would bring her no more love at the dinner table than they'd show for her cousin Dom, who'd fart through the meal with impunity, who juggled thirty years of tobacco in his throat whenever he laughed, and who sat fallow for six straight months every year, waiting for the grass he would cut all summer to start growing again from under the snow. Such was her parents' capacity for a love unencumbered by the toxicity of settler judgment, a capacity she never felt she inherited, or was able, despite all of the examples around her, to intuit; to love all that was there simply because it was there, and because it had survived.

When Carl tried to kiss her that night before she got into the cab, Sarah just turned, let his nose brush against her cheek as she muttered a word under her breath, a word he would try to remember to look up from the comfort of his own home. He would open the comprehensive dictionary, and land on what he thought meant something like "the ice is breaking up and floating toward here." But with his rudimentary colonial tools, he would not be able to break the word down to its composite parts. He would flip through the pages and feel himself forcing the issue. Feel those parts of himself he hated most emerging.

The rain started outside. It would not stop for seventy-six more days.

⁓❦

More than two years and billions of dollars in federal relief were required before the citizens of Freshet and Long Cross began to feel less like eels who were dying of an unnamed illness and more like citizens again. Those who already lived on the hill were now owners of waterfront property (that is, if the electrical and sewer grids weren't permanently damaged), and many citizens had new living arrangements that included family and friends who had lost their homes outright. About 50 percent of Long Cross remained, about 50 percent of Freshet. A number of hotels on the highway at the top of the hill had been repurposed into affordable housing units. Big box stores became central hubs. Parking lots, used less often now because more citizens were in walking distance from where they lodged, were repurposed as outdoor markets in order to give some semblance of the time before. Most of the makers in the town became salvage artists.

It all happened fast, too fast. But people were adapting. Only one year later, on a remote conference call, did the municipal government turn its attention to ways of meaningfully engaging with the drowned parts of the city that, studies were showing, were never again to emerge.

⁓❦

Sarah's family would provide a number of traditional canoes to transport the city's Elders and dignitaries to where the concert would be performed. Anyone who had a non-motorized aquatic vessel was invited to attend. Turtle Island's most famous opera singer and composer was going to perform their now classic piece, named after the carapace of a water beetle, and sung in the traditional language. Carl remembered them performing it a few years back at the newly opened opera house. Playing a grand piano, there was a moment when they stood up on the bench, looked into the piano's belly and projected their voice into the soundboard. Carl and the other audience members could hear their voice ride through the wood grain, project outward from the other end of the piano. It was drugs, thought Carl, by which he meant spiritual. Tonight, this performer would actually be singing from inside a three-hundred-year-old canoe, around the fiddlehead-engraved spire, the lone remaining section of the opera house not underwater. Carl paddled out with his family as Sarah paddled out with hers.

Carl took no pleasure at all in having been right. He had been called to the task, along with everyone else in Freshet and Long Cross, of reorganizing after the floods. The work took every part of his body: mind, muscle memory, beating heart. Abstract ideas mingled with basic generosities. Things that he used to call grunt work sometimes became his work too. He was out of the office, waist-deep in reality. It was cold. It was sometimes toxic. But it felt good to move.

Only now, as the singer's voice carried over the water, over the floating tea lights and the faces of his neighbours, did Carl catch a glimpse of a man he was sure was one of the BMX kids, now in his twenties, in a canoe with what looked like his wife and daughter, a girl of six or seven, who sat between her parents in the middle of the canoe. Then Carl looked down into the water beside him and saw something. A bit of the old pride returned, and it made him sick. The little girl, too, saw something in the water. But the adults in the canoe both reminded her of the dangers lurking there, and implored her to sit back down. She rolled her eyes at them, almost in a full revolution. Lost her balance for half a second, then steadied herself inside the hull.

NOTES ON A VERSION OF *THE WASTE LAND*

I

The first thing one notices about F is the extensive padding of each of his pockets. Protruding from various points of his collared denim shirt and safari vest are the tops of small notepads, pens, folded pages torn from magazines and newspapers, even a passport (though he resides permanently here in the state hospital, and, if on a day pass, must return to his chambers by nine or risk being kicked out). He will, during our weekly meetings, usually bring along one or two plastic Strand bags filled with complete issues of *Le Monde*, back issues of Sotheby's auction house catalogues, pamphlets advertising readings at New York University or events at the public library, maybe some notices of philosophy, psychology or literature conferences in faraway places like Vancouver or Hamburg (places one assumes he has neither the means nor the permission from nurses and doctors to go to), and of course—scrawled out in Spanish, French, English and occasionally Portuguese—pages and pages of his own handwritten poems.

He arrives about fifteen minutes late, after my second reminder call of the morning. I'm at our usual spot, a table inside the Subway sandwich restaurant. The "restaurant" is inside the hospital, directly across from a horticultural therapy centre that I've rarely seen anyone come in or out of, though I've sat at this exact spot every week for close to sixteen months. The Subway is the only dining alternative to the cafeteria, and, while mostly populated by doctors and nurses, there are usually two or three other patients around. I think F likes it here because it is the place inside the hospital that most approximates the city. It has a red neon

OPEN sign. It has wall-sized photos of fresh tomatoes and cucumbers. The sharp tang in the air is the same you'd find in the Subway restaurants in Flatbush or Times Square.

I have never actually seen the cafeteria. I'd also never, until the end of my time as a teaching fellow, seen F's living quarters. As per stipulation in the Goldwater Hospital Writers handbook, I also don't know the specifics of his diagnosis and condition. As for F, he doesn't have any idea that, after volunteering for six months, I am now being paid by the university to be here. I wouldn't tell him because I think that we have become friends, and it would hurt his pride. In a way, it hurts mine. There's our table in Subway. There's one hour a week to discuss his poems or art or, more often, the state of his life in general. This is what we have.

Me: "F, how are you?"

Him: "Good and bad."

Me: "Oh yeah?"

"Kafkanation machinations," he says, and bursts out laughing. This robust laugh usually punctuates either an instance of wordplay, or one of the many moments when I shake my head and look up blankly as he brings up an author or critic like Christine Brooke-Rose or Lou Andreas-Salomé, whom I'd never heard of before. I write these names down in my notebook.

"The nurses," he says, "are giving me problems."

He goes on to explain an elaborate game of cat and mouse wherein the nurses, when he is away from his room, are sneaking in to remove his extensive collection of books and papers and move them down to storage. Storage, he tells me, is unlocked and open to any patient, and he is quite sure the other patients are stealing his books and selling them for drug money. It isn't uncommon for F to finish our meeting by handing me a stack of his poems and saying, "Hold on to these. I don't trust the people here."

F has, by his own admission, been in some kind of psychotherapy for thirty years. He claims to have been at the Coler-Goldwater Hospital for only a year, but I have been seeing him for longer than that already. From our weekly conversations, I learn that he grew up in a farmhouse on a large mango grove in the Dominican Republic. From there he went on to study psychology and what he terms "the sociology of literature" at the Universidad Complutense de Madrid and the Sorbonne Nouvelle in Paris. He then returned to the Dominican Republic to work as a library researcher, translate the poetry of T.S. Eliot into Spanish, and—this part I'd learn from his translator's bio—teach in the faculty of humanities at the Universidad Autónoma de Santo Domingo. He then moved with his family to New York City, after which the details become unclear. I think his three grown children still live in the United States. Three or four times he has mentioned a recent call or afternoon visit from one of them. He once pulled a letter-sized, plastic-covered photograph out of a stack of poems and papers. The photograph was of a smiling young woman wearing a bright-red sweater. "My greatest work!" he exclaimed. Then he laughed again, and sighed.

~&

I express my sympathy for his storage issues. He pulls out a pair of black reading glasses. Last week he had a pair of red glasses. Both pairs are missing right arms. I mention this to him. "Somebody is performing some kind of witchcraft on my glasses," he says. He rifles through a stack of paper, settles on three or four pages and sets the black pair at an odd angle atop his nose. I ask if the hospital gift shop might have a glasses repair kit of some kind. "No" he says, "but I think perhaps I can use a small piece of string."

II

There were other members of the hospital writing workshop whose symptoms were more outwardly visible than F's. He was the most sophisticated writer and reader in the class. He was also the most ready and articulate critic of the workshop itself, and on many days appeared to hate the exercises that he viewed as beneath him and his abilities, making his displeasure known.

The Coler-Goldwater Hospital was on Roosevelt Island, a small bit of land in the East River between Brooklyn and Manhattan. The place had been home to both an asylum and a smallpox hospital prior to Coler-Goldwater's opening in 1939. Ten years ago, there were about twelve thousand residents on this island, many living in the then new condo developments that I would pass each week on my walk from the subway station at the centre of the island toward its southern tip. The hospital, divided into the Coler segment on the northern tip and the Goldwater segment on the south, had 998 total beds, meaning that patients made up approximately one twelfth of the island population. The Coler-Goldwater Hospital was on a very coveted piece of land. The views of Manhattan were spectacular. Around 2008, Stanford University was supposedly in talks with Mayor Bloomberg about turning this section of the hospital into an engineering school. By 2013, the hospital was gone.

Because F is a sophisticated writer and reader, because he is so often more lucid in conversation than some of the other participants, because he claims to have been the first person in the Caribbean to translate the complete poems of T.S. Eliot into Spanish, I venture that he has stared out from somewhere on the hospital grounds toward the skyline, recalling passages from Eliot's *Waste Land* that he knows so well, perhaps comparing the rat who "crept softly through the vegetation /

Dragging its slimy belly on the bank" with the rats along the East River, "The sound of horns and motors" with the deafening noise of traffic from the FDR Drive and on the Queensboro Bridge overhead.

"River suddenly passed by / a few pages sleepwalking / in a TV show," F says, in his own words, in his own poem.

~&

Eliot's "Unreal City" in *The Waste Land* is London. It was written during a well-documented difficult stage in T.S. Eliot's life and in his marriage. Eliot struggled throughout his life with his own nervous disorders. In the earliest days of the 1920s, he was working at a bank, and was otherwise occupied with numerous articles and book reviews as he tried to establish his literary reputation. His first wife, Vivienne, suffered from her own, often more acute, disorders. (She would eventually, and controversially, spend the final nine years of her life institutionalized.) His letters around this period, collected in *The Letters of T.S. Eliot: Volume 1* (Yale University Press, 2011), reveal a broken-down, exhausted Eliot. Vivienne's father had been struck with a grave illness, which further exacerbated things at home. In a letter dated October 3, 1921, Eliot writes to his older brother:

> I have been feeling nervous and shaky lately and have
> little self-control... [the specialist] examined me... and
> said I had greatly overdrawn my nervous energy, and
> must go straight away for three months complete rest and
> change and must live according to a strict regimen which
> he has prescribed... I confess I dread this enforced rest
> and solitude... and expect a period of great depression.

Not a month later, at seaside rest in Cliftonville, Kent, Eliot wrote to his friend Sydney Schiff with news that part three of his poem *The Waste*

Land had been drafted. Sly references are made to famous lines ("I can connect / Nothing with nothing") and symbols from the section, as well as to the spell of fragmented civic and sensory experience that section three evokes: "I have written only some fifty lines, and have read nothing, literally—I sketch the people, after a fashion, and practise scales on the mandoline." Two days later, still resting, writing the poem he had previously been unable to find the time or energy to undergo, he is happier, certain, as he says in a letter to his friend Richard Aldington, that "my nerves are a mild affair, due, not to overwork, but an aboulie and emotional derangement which has been a lifelong affliction."

III

If *The Waste Land* has a central character, it is the blind prophet Tiresias, a man who has spent some time as a woman, who has been to Hades, who is a harbinger that speaks in epigrams and misdirection and rarely reveals—though he has seen some things—the whole extent of what he's seen. He is described in section three as "throbbing between two lives," a nod to his narrative omniscience, sexual omniscience, his ability to shuttle between life and death, his ability to recognize the small house agent clerk returning home as an Odysseus apposite, while at the same time satirizing Odysseus's return in an impotent scene of contemporary domestic life. Tiresias, in Eliot's poem, experiences his city and his time at a dissonant remove, internalizes the city's architecture, pollution and cacophony. Stasis and suffering are enduring conditions, even as Tiresias shuttles between worlds and times. There is the overriding sense, however objectively false, that the world has oppressed his own consciousness in particular: "O Lord Thou pluckest me out / O Lord Thou pluckest // burning."

In addition to listening to his stories and transcribing his poems, I spent my time with F negotiating what I perceived in myself as two different conditions: the first was the enormous respect that I had for his lifetime of reading and thinking, an ability to read and write in four different languages, for the curiosity and dogged ambition he maintained in an environment where men and women would often be forced, by things outside of their control, to give up. The second was the frustration I felt on account of his unwillingness to participate, in spite of his perfect attendance, in 90 percent of the outlined writing exercises we had created for the class. There was his insistence on delivering a short lecture on something at best only tangentially related to any questions or comments about the poems presented. Alone together during our meetings, he took a thrill in showing his young writing partner up in some area or another of literary expertise. I can still hear that laugh as I type this. But in the Coler-Goldwater Hospital, stripped of a great deal of your own autonomy, forced to navigate your various passions with people who approached art for primarily social or therapeutic reasons, of course you would try to combat that process, to make these sly plays for power.

And so I listened to him talk. I took the sheaves of crumpled pages he presented me and offered, in the one language I knew fluently, to be a second set of eyes. I offered to submit some of his work to the graduate student journal's special international issue, and the editors enthusiastically chose two of his poems for publication. I offered to type every poem he gave me on the computer, to print them out and give them back to him the following week. In subsequent weeks he would complain of no longer having the printouts. They were stolen. *Kafkanation machinations*. Would I see if I still had them on my computer? Would I be able to print them out for him again?

And often during our one-on-one visits in the Subway restaurant we would be interrupted. Sometimes it was by the hospital's resident Catholic priest, a man F respected and admired. Sometimes it was by patients in more immediately visible states of pain than F, asking for change. Someone in the hallway would occasionally throw a fit, which is probably the wrong word; someone would occasionally scream in a way that I could not translate, perhaps at the sheer indignity that can occur in being alive. F would close his eyes and press a finger to his forehead, occasionally shaking, occasionally opening his eyes again to shout back at whomever it was, imploring them to keep it down.

IV

Flebas el fenicio, muerto hace quince días
Olvido el grito de las gaviotas, y la profunda oleada del mar
y las pérdidas y las ganancias.
Una corriente submarina
Recogió sus huesos en susurro, mientras se levantaba y caía
Paso las etapas de suedad y juventud
Entrando el remolino.
Gentil o judío tu
Oh tú que das vuelta a la rueda y miras hacia el viento,
Considera a Flebas, quien fué una vez hermoso y alto
como tú.

—"Death by Water," *Poesía Completa*, T.S. Eliot, translated by
    Fernando Vargas

V

It was during one of our last individual visits that F suggested I come upstairs to the residence so he could show me some papers he had forgotten to bring downstairs. I had not inquired about seeing the residence beforehand, but had, on the occasions when I'd imagined him deep in thought, naively pictured him at a little desk by a window look-ing out over the river. Medical accoutrements would probably be the dominant theme of the modest room, but perhaps there would be a small shelf bursting at the seams with books and papers, something like an X-rayed version of his safari vest, as well as a picture on the wall of his children and wife from their first year in New York or from earlier, happier times in the Dominican Republic.

~&~

The hallways were busier upstairs than on the main floor. F had a bounce in his step, was in an agreeable mood. This was often the case on the last day before an extended break from the workshop: his guard would be down; he wanted to be remembered fondly and thought upon during these breaks, and he'd often call me from a public phone in the hospital to ask what my wife and I were up to during my time away.

On the way to his room we passed a paraplegic man in an electric wheelchair. F swung around, removed a small piece of chocolate from a silver packet and placed it directly onto the man's tongue.

F's jovial demeanour that day puts me in mind of the letter Eliot wrote to his friend Mary Hutchinson while under the care of a new specialist in Switzerland. *The Waste Land* had been drafted and he was awaiting Ezra Pound's now famous edit in the New Year: "This is a very quiet town, except when the children come down hill on scooters over the cobbles. Mostly banks and chocolate shops. Good orchestra plays 'The Love Nest.' A horse fell down yesterday; one cannot see the moun-tains, too foggy. How are you?"

The closest approximation of this giddiness in the poem itself might be the rooster call in the final section: "Co co rico co co rico."

~&~

The room is far worse than I had imagined. He shares it with three other patients. There are two beds on either side of the room. The two beds paired on each side are inches from one another, and there is only a thin blue curtain that one can pull around each bed in order to get some semblance of privacy. He has an ancient, miniature television set suspended above the bed by a white mechanical arm. There's an end table beside the bed so towering with garbage that I sympathize with the nurses—who were meant to keep the place in some sort of order—as much as I do with F, who keeps "losing" his things. The bed is unmade. He is in a hurry to find what he wants to show me. He lifts up his pillow.

It's a photocopied version of T.S. Eliot's *Poesía Completa*, cover image included, stapled together, yellowed at the edges, which he has been hiding from the nurses, and sleeping on top of at night. F's prologue ends abruptly after a discussion of *The Waste Land*, on a note about Eliot's hard work and his crisis at home, and doesn't pick up again to discuss how, after a long fallow period, Eliot managed to write his later works.

III

IF IT GETS QUIET LATER ON, I WILL MAKE A DISPLAY

I was still working at Book City Bloor West Village when Paul Vermeersch helped see my first slim volume of poems through to print. One of my favourite things in those early days was to watch customers interact with the small pile of copies of my book on the table. Which is to say, something in me needed to silently observe the degree to which this book was ignored in favour of so many other sensible purchases. I watched without ever mentioning to anyone looking that the book was mine. These observations allowed me to rightsize my expectations, to physically acknowledge the tiny niche my own words occupied among the cities and forests of other words. For I had grown up in a privileged version of the world where I always just assumed my voice *already* mattered, before I had any real thoughts or ideas in my head. This assumption began to crack almost as soon as I began sharing my poems with any sort of public.

And yet the blood-flowing charge of having even just a few stanzas around in the cities and forests of books has remained, for me, a lifegiving force. And the odd evening (we're talking two or three times) when someone would pick up my book, read and add it to a pile of other books felt equivalent to the other surprising and life-changing connections I was making during my time at the store. These exchanges culminated one evening when Sue and I, who had by now been going for walks and sharing poems outside of our shifts for a number of months, stared across the table from one another in the Victory Cafe, and I felt some kind of new understanding between us enter my very bones.

I DON'T WASTE my time at the Fredericton store as a voyeur of my own titles these days. Without question, my favourite thing to do now during my Sunday-afternoon shift is to collect and display other books in the windows and on the tables. Kalpna is the aspirational figure to my amateur forays into this form of poetry. I don't have her skillset, but I am completely immersed in my attempts at the genre. Because I work that afternoon shift on my own, my manager will sometimes leave a note: *If it gets quiet later on, can you make a display featuring...*, but more often than not I am given free rein. The process is physical and associative (two tables side by side labelled "the Fast Lane" and "the Slow Lane," for example, or a display simply called "All-Consuming"), requiring a quick distillation of organizing principles. How do you bring self-help in contact with fiction? How do you bring Indigenous literatures in contact with the how-to books? If a boreal display is to be made, as is often called for in a place like Fredericton, one might layer the display in the ways the forest is layered. A lowermost layer will include books about the ground beneath our feet, Robert Macfarlane's *Underland*, for example, but the subsoil might also include *The Worm* by Elise Gravel, from her Disgusting Critters series for kids. A second ground-layer level could include *Medicine Walk* by the late Richard Wagamese set next to a guide to the local hiking trails, both a short walk from Rebecca Solnit's *A Field Guide to Getting Lost*. There will be a canopy of popular tree books, or storybooks featuring trees on their covers, the taller the better, nestled at the back, towering over the ground layer. Then, on the shelf that backs onto the display window, another available layer for birdwatching books, to which I'd add *The Cloudspotter's Guide* by Gavin Pretor-Pinney. Hours dissolve. Pleasures interlock. There are days when this task feels like writing, or at least like Thoreau might have felt watching bubbles form under the ice in spring, making the ice "crack and whoop."

THERE WAS ONCE a customer at Book City Bloor West Village who approached me at the cash desk, not to ask me for a recommendation, not to purchase a book, but to tell me, with that buttoned-down, marble-countered Bay Street glow—that I had affixed myself to an industry on the cusp of death. "Nobody is going to read books anymore," he said, staring straight into my eyes. "You know this, don't you? None of this is going to matter in a couple of years, none of it." He left waving his hand dismissively at me.

A few surviving bookstores, like the one I find myself working at in Fredericton some sixteen years after that exchange, have continued to operate in these Amazon-infused deadfalls for a couple of decades now. It's still very easy to connect the anxiety about the survival of bookstores with anxieties about the survival of everything else in our world. It is particularly true in our time of global warming and mass extinction, while the forests are burning at a rate we have never seen, or as a new century's pandemic threatens so many businesses month to month, purchase to purchase, and airborne droplets threaten the very lives of those who choose to work in and patronize these stores.

Having worked myself into an anxious state, longing for an immediate slowdown, I will sometimes return to a book of poems called *Heroin*, by writer and New York resident Charlie Smith. His poem "As for Trees" reads in a manner similar to the urban quick-hit-list style of O'Hara's "A Step Away from Them." But Smith's poem is not celebratory. It's as if the speaker were waking up in his city apartment, sweaty, drug-sick and struck with the sudden realization that for some years now he's been utterly removed from the forest. It's as if he is desperately trying to make up for this absence by listing every urban tree he's ever encountered or thought of before in his life—"duplicitous conifers," "questing pines," "forthright pistachios"—affixing to them the paranoid baggage of addiction: "The obstinate oaks, the complicated stirring of the honey locust, / There are catkins and bouquets, single florets dipped in wax." These sorts of inventories have, for me, a rhythm that soothes. But with that soothing often comes a moment similar to that of a blackout or a doomscroll, when such descriptions start to feel like pacification, like I am simply feeding the many-limbed material of the world into the furnace between my ears, counterintuitively fuelling the fears that I can no longer remove myself from and that I can no longer act within. "As for Trees" has always read to me as purposefully mimetic of a certain species of obsessiveness, one step removed, as language, from the violence inherent in conspicuous consumption. This poem reminds me why, as a writer, as a bookseller, as a person, I inhabit myself most fully when I am around many different kinds of books, or different kinds of art, or different kinds of trees. Taking my first job at the bookstore in Toronto, I think, was the beginning of that understanding. There was a gravitational force to the little store that I could not do without.

TOWARD THE END of *The Odd Woman and the City*, Vivian Gornick narrates the moment when she handed her manuscript in progress over to a friend, who, reading it, charged her with the sin of romanticizing the city, while at the same time ignoring that "seventy-five percent of [New York City's] manufacturing base" had been forced, by the hands of global capitalism, to leave for elsewhere.

In the City of Stately Elms (but also hemlocks, birches, pin cherries, maples...), as the faculty spouse of a person with a tenured job, I am aware that I can be picky about what kind of work I choose for myself with the time leftover from household tasks. I have the luxury of getting a little romantic about my Sunday afternoon at the store. One of the more fascinating parts of this time in my life as homemaker and part-time bookseller is that I am constantly coming up against prejudices rooted deep in my own person, how strong a hold the idea that earning both financial and social capital are the true measurements of a life well lived. And I get to experience, after all of those financially tenuous but occasionally thrilling years in the cities (and bookstores) of New York, Toronto, Calgary, Madrid and Montreal, how easily life becomes isolated for the one packing the lunches and fretting about the closeness of the branches to the house in the university town.

Literature has always, among its many uses, been a stay against the quiet, branch-breaking bitterness and narrowing of the spirit that certain kinds of loneliness can engender. It is also why people still come to the bookstore to mill around and browse the shelves on a Sunday afternoon. I see them every week. I recommend the latest Esi Edugyan, André Alexis, Rachel Cusk...

And each and every year when I am tasked with making the autumnal display, taping plastic orange and red leaves to the window to set against the leaves falling from the maples outside, I centre a book that sheds more light on the day-to-day aspects of the display maker than any other work I know. The book is the 2012 catalogue of the paintings of Mary Pratt, who grew up in a house just a few minutes' walk from the store. The cover is a painting of three jars of fall preserves, called *Jelly Shelf*. It is lit from within with the light that only Mary Pratt could paint. In the jars she had seen a light that reminded her of what shone through the stained glass of Wilmot United Church (which is also just around the corner from the store). But the analogy for that light I've turned to lately is one from the mycorrhizal network. Namely, it reminds me of those little orange jelly mushrooms, *Dacrymyces palmatus*, that I sometimes find growing around the rotting stumps on my walks in the nearby park. These mushrooms reminded the kids at my child's pre-school of the neon orange of Kraft Dinner, so they dubbed them "macaroni mushrooms." The light in the jars is like this jelly-mushroom light, and after you place the book in the middle of the window, the rest of the display just starts to order itself.

The Pratt catalogue, being a few years old, sells slowly. A bit of extra movement after she died in 2018, but otherwise just a single copy every now and again (forty-three in ten years, to be precise). But three or four times in the past five years, I've returned to work the following week to find it's been purchased out of the window, and these are some of my good days out in the world.

IN OUR FIRST year in the City of Stately Elms, when my tree anxiety was at its height, a new wing was opened at the local art gallery—more a tall-ceilinged cube than a wing—perched over the banks of the river known as Wolastoq. The inaugural exhibition in this cube was none other than Thaddeus Holownia's 24 *Tree Studies for Henry David Thoreau*. There they were again seven years later, transported from the Armory Show in New York and towering over the clean new windows and the pristinely waxed new floor. Seeing the series again, I felt the same sense of relief I felt upon that first encounter. These were trees that wouldn't catch fire or collapse or create runways for rodents. These weren't fossilized remains of that brief time in New York, but were living somehow, seemingly rising back up to tell me that I lived here in Fredericton now, and the trees in my own backyard were not to be feared or ignored. To labour the image of those trees even further, at Bookends, the second-hand bookstore across the river, three years after the gallery opening, I came upon the 2004 catalogue for an exhibit called *Walden Pond Revisited*. It was designed by Andrew Steeves of Gaspereau Press and by the artist Thaddeus Holownia, published to celebrate Thaddeus's Corkin Shopland Gallery exhibit in Toronto, Ontario. So those trees were actually on display in Toronto too, the whole time I stood sweating outside the hotel or was stumbling through Kensington Market at four a.m. Not only 24 *Tree Studies for Henry David Thoreau*, but also *Vernal Pool Near Wyman's Meadow*, and a phantom fish under the newly thawing water, and another bit of slowly breaking ice, and a centrifugal split in the centre of the pond, blood-vessel trails in the ice which made the whole pond look like a human eye. I ask the bookseller if she might consider docking the somewhat prohibitive fifty-dollar price tag. Seeing the rest of the woodpile my family of readers has hefted up onto the desk, and knowing what every good bookseller knows, she drops the cost to twenty-five.

SOMETIMES, IF IT gets quiet at the store, I daydream. I have brought the oligarch's forty suitcases downstairs to an out-of-the-way corner of the lobby. Instead of racing through the hallways, the restaurant, the upstairs patio in search of the man who would pay me an equitable amount for my labour, I remain in place. I wipe my brow, grab a drink of water, and begin to open up one of the suitcases, quietly leafing through layers of expensive clothes and souvenirs. Then I open the next, then the next. The task takes hours. Takes days. Takes years. Nobody—not the assistant, not the bodyguard, not the manager of the hotel—ever bothers me. I have the do-not-disturb-me air of someone quietly reading books.

HERE IS A display for these pages only: aimed at the general reader, but personal, and incomplete, and common as bubbles in ice. For the idea of the bookstore as a wooded sheltering place, see *Walden; or, Life in the Woods*, by Henry David Thoreau. For the intelligence of other species and the scientific proof of our interconnectedness: *Finding the Mother Tree* by Suzanne Simard or *Braiding Sweetgrass* by Robin Wall Kimmerer. For the sudden rush of insight, interaction and image on a city street, *The Collected Poems of Frank O'Hara*, edited by Donald Allen. For the essential history of the bookstore as social experiment, theatre and community hub, see *The Bookseller's Tale* by Martin Latham. For bookselling against tyranny and oppression, in the name of equal rights for all, see *David Ruggles: A Radical Black Abolitionist and the Underground Railroad in New York City* by Graham Russell Gao Hodges. For the need to stave off loneliness and to remain visible among the local population—be they trees or people or both—there's a copy of *The Odd Woman and the City* by Vivian Gornick. For the shadowy dealers of books: *Between Parentheses* by Roberto Bolaño. For the effect of their drugs: *Heroin* by Charlie Smith. To understand that your tree is also "Everybody's Tree": *Poems About Trees*, edited by Harry Thomas. For nutrients that are stored in the eye and the mind and the brush: *Mary Pratt*, with contributions from Ray Cronin, Mireille Eagan et al. And finally, a copy of *Walden Pond Revisited* by Thaddeus Holownia, for new titles reawaken the formative texts.

Actual displays at the store will, of course, be made mostly of books I have yet to read. I consider the covers, the colours, the words in the titles and the themes. Only the vaguest trace of authorship exists when I'm putting these displays together; I trust the work of the people who felled the trees, who manufactured the paper, the authors of the books, the editors, the designers, the marketers, the browsers' own tastes and desire for knowledge. I like being there among those who linger. I offer assistance at the door upon entering, but then only when asked. And then, after they've come to their decisions, and when one of those plastic book stands is empty, I feel like we've both made a bit of room for more energy to enter. The book is carried out into the world, and I place a new one on the stand. I sweep up the leaves on the floor.

J was awaiting the start of her Monday shift in the break room, the requisite one person per table, pulling her mask on and off her chin between sips from a coffee thermos brought from home, awaiting word from the high command.

Epilogue Books, the global chain in whose suburban Halifax location she worked, was, like the rest of the world, in a state of crisis. J and her co-workers were the lucky ones, or so they were constantly being told by the high command. Apart from a few circuit-breaking lockdowns lasting two to three weeks, the store had remained open over the course of the year; case numbers in the relatively isolated eastern provinces remained manageable. A few of the worried older staff members and young folks who were just working to get their parents off their backs left the team. Sixteen of the twenty-five Epilogue Halifax employees, creepily referred to by the high command as the "spines" of the organization, had kept their jobs.

Ten spines remained on the floor for each daytime shift, and ten customers at a time would be allowed in the store. This created a strange sensation of coldness in a store that could already, in spite of having three thousand square feet devoted entirely to blankets and candles, be accused of being chilly.

The rules for wave three of pandemic protocol appeared on the break-room TV screen:

1. One spine will remain at the entranceway from the parking lot, demanding each customer answer the twenty-two-question survey, sanitize and log their contact information in the book.
2. Two spines will remain on the cash registers.
3. One spine will continue to operate the quick-dry sanitization drone, flying in crop-row formation from the northwest to southeast corners of the store.

4. The Bean Tryin' Cafe will remain closed, barbed wire affixed to both the chairs and tables.
5. The entranceway from the interior of Champions Mall will remain closed.
6. The remaining six spines will patrol the floor and ensure that no customer touches any item they are not prepared to purchase.
7. Spines will offer their assistance to every customer showing interest in a particular book or item, including handling, but also reading opening paragraphs and tables of contents, at a distance of three metres and through their handheld megaphones.
8. Whenever the customer refuses this assistance, force may be used to prevent indiscriminate browsing. Weapons will be provided to spines for this purpose.
9. These weapons are to be returned to the holds shelf, and sanitized each night by the cleaning staff.

J had to reread them a second and third time to be sure they were real. She looked around the room to try to make eye contact with her fellow staff, to address the absurdity of what was being proposed, but, as had been true for months now, no spine would offer her anything like contact, even with their eyes. The pandemic had been going on for some time now, and everyone was just keeping their heads down at this point, trying to make it through each day.

J and her fellow spines finished their beverages, checked the battery levels of their megaphones, washed their hands, and lined up at the door, where a metal case of weaponry had been forklifted onto the shop floor. It appeared that most of the weapons had been acquired via police and military surplus auctions: tasers, batons, green-handled hunting blades... J considered a semi-automatic rifle for a while, figuring the sheer gaudiness of this weapon would relieve her of any uncomfortable aggression from the customers. But then she looked a little further down...

Where Epilogue's high command would acquire medieval weaponry was beyond her. But the resources of the high command were limitless. Sizeable donations to important public projects no doubt created unforeseen weak spots in the law during a time of crisis, ones that had allowed high command to arm its spines, who were now doing actual harm to a customer base that, even before the pandemic, high command had aggressively (some would say violently) encouraged to shop online.

J twirled the morning star in her hand, gave it a few exaggeratedly slow home-run swings, then attached it to its accompanying shoulder harness. She was trying to keep things light and bright, but deep inside her she knew she'd been conscripted into something that she wasn't quite prepared for. None of the spines were. Nevertheless, when Norah Jones' "The Nearness of You" came on over the loudspeaker, it was time to begin the shift.

J was stationed in the stuffed animals and games area for the first couple of days that week, which was more or less a cakewalk. Parents rarely showed up at the store with their kids these days, abiding to a one-family-member shopping policy. When they did, a certain excess of surveillance was already ingrained in the process—parents hovering, imploring, grabbing wrists and basically ensuring that anything unnecessary was not touched. The board games and puzzles were boxed, wrapped in plastic, their contents pretty much evident from the pictures, while the otters, elephants and mythical creatures just stared out from the shelves with their oversized eyes.

On Thursday J was assigned to a small area covering entertainment, science, belles lettres, religion and philosophy, and knew she was in for a tough time. This area had once been referred to as "dawdlers row," and it still received its share of indecisive folks, people who confused Epilogue with a lending library. Her co-worker Wren had horribly injured a customer's leg, deploying a crossbow on a man who had refused to commit to purchasing the finger-soiled copy of *Gravity and Grace*. And apparently Tomas, who'd been edgy and anxious for months, sensing a size advantage against a man reading a book about gut chemistry (with his mask down under his nose no less), had put his semi-automatic gun down and went at the guy with his fists, "a little too gleefully," as his suspension report—published in the weekly staff newsletter—declared.

J approached the woman standing close to the shelf—slowly, so as not to frighten her.

"I can read that to you."

"Huh?"

"That book you are eyeing. I can stand three metres away from you and read parts of it to you. I can use my megaphone if you're hard of hearing. I have these plastic gloves."

The middle-aged woman backed away a few steps from the shelf. She looked intently at J's eyes, at her headband, at her blue Epilogue Books staff vest. She looked at the handle of the morning star peaking over J's shoulder. J had been claiming the same weapon each morning, growing more and more comfortable with the idea it was something she'd have to use.

"Have you read this one?"

"I have not."

"Then yes, I think you should read it to me. That would be very nice."

The woman set the book down flat on the shelf and backed up seven paces, so that J could walk over and pick it up to read. J made sure her mask was squarely over her mouth, flipped on the switch of her amplification device, and began.

Her voice sounded slightly auto-tuned, but the microphone worked. The story she read to the woman was by a Frenchman, written when he was very young, and happened to describe, if you would believe it, a bookseller. J loved these serendipitous moments. Sometimes when she struggled with depression, or just couldn't figure out what to eat for lunch, she would comb the shelves for signs.

From what she could glean from the archaic style of the prose, the bookseller was a former monk from Spain. Jury was out on whether he could actually read, but the man *loved* books. Just putting his hands on the shelves would set his body trembling. "It was not learning that he loved, it was its expression," she read aloud to the woman. "He loved a book because it was a book; he loved its odour, its form, its title."

The woman asked J to continue to the very end of the story, which was not long. J felt an exchange of energy was happening between her and this customer, something she hadn't even noticed through the pandemic that she was missing. J continued. The woman's eyes were closed. Her hands clutched at the lapels of her beige suede coat.

The monk killed another man who outbid him on a book, "a Latin Bible, with Greek commentaries." He burned the successful collector's store to the ground, ran into the blaze to retrieve the book he had been outbid on, and left his competitor trapped inside to die. There were more and more crimes each day, "and all seemed to come from an invisible hand. It was a dagger suspended over every roof and over every family." A hired spy, called the Prosecutor, eventually clued in to the bookseller's guilt, finding the common thread between the crimes. J loved the description the Prosecutor gave while delivering his report: "It was with difficulty that one could distinguish the principal action from the parentheses and repetitions." Those were the very same difficulties of her days, thought J, the very same difficulties of her thoughts.

The bookseller is sentenced to death by the courts, yet seems calm about the decision. Asks only that his library remain intact, "be given to the man who has the most books..."

The story ended. The woman opened her eyes. There was silence. J spoke up.

"I can bring this up to the cash register if you're done."

"No, I don't think that will be necessary."

Then the woman's eyes began to comb the shelves, reading the sections aloud as she encountered them. A couple of seconds lapsed between the words *poetry* and *literary criticism*. Maybe another two between *philosophy* and *visual art*. *Drama* at this point was two L-shaped brackets basically holding hands over five or six slim volumes. The woman couldn't bring herself to say the heading aloud. Instead she turned back to J, opening her coat and revealing a weapon that J did not recognize, that had never appeared among any of those available to the spines.

For the last few months J had done nothing but come to Epilogue for work and go home at night. She shopped for groceries once a week. She had been dutifully following all corporate and government health and safety instructions. She had a friend in Ontario whose grandfather had died. J had listened to her friend cry over the phone. She knew the virus to be real.

Nevertheless, this woman in front of her, who held J's gaze as she crouched down in what almost seemed like a meditative pose, was also real. And J knew that only one of them was leaving the store that afternoon alive. So she crouched in turn, as the contemporary jazz in the background faded in her ears, became one long and constant ring. The drone flew in formation over both of their heads, raining a gentle, slightly toxic mist.

THE GAFFER AND THE MORNING STAR

It was a sort of toy house; no walls, framed out of thin wooden poles. The interior was big enough for a throw cushion, and the structure was tall enough for an adult to sit down in comfortably (most likely to meditate). It occupied the corner of the living room where two floor-to-ceiling windows met. The view outside—the harbour, the imposing city skyline and its many lights—moved right through the frame. The apartment was a secondary residence, used full-time for only one academic semester each year. It was one of those modern, sterile places where the owners could afford to be judicious about what they brought to the setting. The lone wall of the living room held no pictures apart from a small oil painting of a scorpion that had been applied to a piece of untreated wood. Nothing else really distinguished it as somewhere lived-in, apart perhaps from the collage of photographs and ticket stubs on the refrigerator, looking blown in from the streets and caught on the cool metal door.

Chance had brought me there. A few hours earlier I was nursing a beer at the bar with my fellow fiction students. I was in the middle of an elaborate tale of a night gone horribly wrong: my then roommate, a gaffer for a reality TV show, arriving home drunk, disrobing, and threatening his girlfriend and a visiting cousin with some kind of weapon he could not have possibly owned, like a war hammer, or a morning star. I had barged, faux-heroically, out of my bedroom only to be told by his girlfriend that they were okay, to please just go back inside my room, where I spent the rest of the night behind the closed door with my phone in my hand, thumb near the emergency icon, body vibrating, listening to the gaffer's threats get slower and directed more toward himself, and to the sound of his bare skin lifting and falling from his leather sectional as he tossed and turned and eventually passed out.

In the morning I packed up some essentials in a gym bag and left, not knowing how or when or if I was going to return.

Before that day's fiction workshop I asked if I could store my bag in May's office at the university. May was responsible for organizing the graduate program's reading events. Three floors down from the administrative higher-ups and the professors, her office was near the kitchen where we snacked. She was the friendliest person on staff. Once, at a crowded reading, she scanned the room for a place for me to sit, walked me up to the front row, ripped from the back of a folding chair a piece of paper bearing the name of the fiction editor of the most prestigious magazine in the country, and told me to sit down. I had so many grand ambitions then, and loved this fabulous edit she had made on the fly.

May wasn't exactly pleased to be saddled with my bag, but said okay, and asked me to tuck it between the cupboard and a three-high stack of boxes full of pamphlets that listed everything going on later that spring. I told her I was going to the bar after class that afternoon, but if she had to leave before I was back, of course she should leave.

I held court over drinks for quite some time. I had a harrowing story to tell, and my fellow fiction writers were eating it up. Beers kept materializing on the table, and at some point my body, which had been shaking all day, stopped shaking. The faces around me kept changing as the evening continued, and eventually the husband of one of our professors, a warm presence at every event, a man whom we just called Odd, arrived at the bar for a quick one. Someone at our table asked him to join us. At the end of maybe my fourth iteration of the story of the naked gaffer—his weapon always changing... a horseman's pick, a katana—Odd left for a minute, returned, put a glass of water on the table in front of me and a set of keys into my hand. He said that he and his husband had a flight in a couple hours for some events in Europe, and that I should use their place while they were away. He hated the idea of the apartment being empty, he said. This was something they did, let people stay in their place while they were gone. He proceeded to write out the address and the directions from the bar. Only seven hours later, smoking alone in front of an all-night pizzeria, did I remember that the piece of paper Odd gave me at the bar was still in my pocket. I was in no condition to confront my present living situation: my small, overpriced room; the remorseful, hungover gaffer and his apologies; his arsenal of imaginary weapons hauled down to street level and left for the curbside economy of second-hand goods.

I sat on the mat in the toy house, in the sterile living room of the apartment, surrounded by skyline. Did the stick-frame house belong to our professor, whose last novel had earned a reported two-million-dollar advance and whose new short story collection was already in talks to be made into a miniseries by a famous Polish director? Or was this place of rest and reflection used most often by Odd, about whom I really knew nothing, who left no written trace, but who always turned up at places where we were, took an interest in us, and who had put the keys to this safe, unoccupied place in my hand?

I got up and started to snoop around, mindful not to open drawers or cupboards, not to be too intrusive, but wanting to see whatever some other visitor here might see. The second bedroom was the fiction writer's office. It too was surprisingly clean, void of the mess of a primary home. There was his desk, his chair and a small window. There was one built-in shelf behind the desk, and on it the complete works of a single author, a woman who wrote voluminous, intricately plotted social novels structured after the migratory patterns of specific mammals and birds. I too had recently been bitten by her work, and this serendipity made me blush. Then I felt a sudden cold shiver and wanted immediately to leave.

I couldn't go back to my old place yet. My toiletries and change of clothes were under lock and key in May's office. So I curled up on the couch under the scorpion painting, and tried to picture Odd and the fiction writer's primary home. It was probably a grand and idiosyncratic place, tucked behind a stand of trees, a house overflowing with books and photographs, blankets, pillows, throw rugs. There'd be a fireplace in the living room that burned all night, a real-life fire, not the facsimile that the lights in the windows of the tall buildings made as they turned on and off, off and on. But what I was really trying to imagine was how people actually lived, their happiness.

Then I woke to the sunrise through the apartment window, through the non-existent walls of the toy house. My phone blinked, a text from the gaffer's girlfriend saying they had driven somewhere upstate for a couple of days, were going to "reflect and unwind." There was a news item in my feed about the fiction writer, to whom the French government had awarded a handsome, "life-altering" financial reward for his body of work thus far.

Dragging my body into the toy house, I took a breath, and closed my eyes. When I opened them again I noticed a substantial spot of blood on the other side of the living room window, which I identified at once as the gaffer's work. Then I circled myself until my wings grew tired, afraid there was no place I'd ever arrive.

Three stories came to mind when I learned that Patrick Lane had died. The first takes place in the introductory buzz of my undergraduate poetry workshop. Twelve people around a conference table, each one probably used to being the solitary, loner scribbler in their communities and families. Each one of us eyeing the others: a herd of moody unicorns. Patrick arrives late, looking, as he takes his seat, to be a shambles. Most of us already have an inkling that making poems is a messy business, and anyone professing to "teach" such an art, some of us figure, must shamble at least as much as they instruct.

Patrick is in the difficult stages of early sobriety. This I would only learn later, after the publication of his memoir *There Is a Season* (McClelland & Stewart, 2004), which confirmed a timeline I sensed as his presence at the head of the table grew steadier from that first-year workshop to the third. Of course, there were rumours swirling around the department and among the students at the bars; rumours I would have been able to confirm outright by reading his personal essay from *Addicted: Notes from the Belly of the Beast*, if I'd been patient enough back then to read anything other than poems.

But on that first day of class he wants to talk about what it's like to see your poems in print, in your very first published collection. He leafs through the volume in front of him as though it were his own debut. He's making sure all the poems are there. He grazes for the first of the typos, which he says one invariably finds. He mimics the deep sigh that follows the first flip through. "Then," he says, in concert with his enactment, "you open the book at random, press your face to the pages, and sniff the length of the spine. And then," he says, closing the book and resting his head on the table, speaking sideways out to the room, "you weep. Because it's all you fucking *have*."

In the second story, Patrick arrives late once again. He's sorry he's late, but we won't believe what he saw. A crow had arrived, in a flurry, on the ledge of his office window. After he and the crow exchanged a brief acknowledgement of each other's presence, the crow turned its attention toward its own claws. It had pinned a wasp to the windowsill and was watching, as Patrick began to watch, the hind end of the wasp wave frantically in the air. Considering the situation for a brief moment, the crow, whose beak is made of hard and durable keratin, removed the stinger with one quick pluck, cast it sideways, and devoured the rest of the wasp.

The third and final story is of a technical nature, concerning the breaking of lines. He and I are in his office, and I am frustrated about some of the comments he has written on my work: the crossing out of whole stanzas, the declarations, double-underlined, that I was writing nothing more than purple prose. I ask, "So then how do you break a line?" He picks up a book. It is his own *Selected Poems: 1977–1997* (Harbour Publishing, 1997). He assures me he is using this simply because it is there. (I'm glad it was.) We go through a number of poems. One of them begins like this:

> There is a moment on the wall when a man looks out
> over the far horizon and wonders when
> they will come. He does not know who they are.
> The wall was built many years ago, long
> before he was born and before his father was
> born. All his life has been spent
> repairing the wall, replacing the fallen
> stones, clearing away the tough grass
> that grows like fingers in the masonry.

What I have to say now is more muscle memory than report. He probably talked about leaving a white space at the end of the first line to emphasize the horizon. He might have talked about end-stopping the third line because the declaration of unknowing must be stated as plainly as possible, unadorned with technique. He might have talked about the perfect summative and metanarrative unit made by the double enjambment that forms "born. All his life has been spent." He might have talked about how the grass as fingers dictates that the stanza must end because as the fingers grow they clutch; they hold the stanza aloft, above whatever follows next.

The subject of "The Great Wall" is a fictional man from Peking (Beijing) who is tasked, over the course of his life, with repairing and maintaining the same section of a wall his father had maintained for the duration of his own.

In tone and subject, this poem is starkly similar to Franz Kafka's story "The Great Wall of China." Kafka's narrator appears to have been employed in the capacity of supervising labourer, overseeing the building of certain sections of the wall:

> Why... did we leave our homes, the stream with its bridges, our mothers and fathers, our weeping wives, our children who needed our care, and depart for the distant city to be trained there, while our thoughts journeyed still farther away to the wall in the north? Why? A question for the high command.

Lane:

> Inside the wall the land is the same
> as outside and once, when he was confused
> by the hot wind, he could not remember
> which side of the wall he lived on and he
> has never forgotten the doubt of that day.

The doubt expressed in the second stanza of Lane's poem is one I've never forgotten, applicable to all forms of conflict in which walls, both real and imagined, are built, maintained or destroyed: walls between people, between cities, between cultures; walls between a person and their own sense of their place within communities local and global. Yet in a rushed, poor first reading I invested too much in the similarities between "The Great Wall" and "The Great Wall of China," to the point where I almost saw Lane performing a kind of intellectual theft.

Kafka's story has been widely cited as a kind of parable of the modernist project in literature. The narrator questions the efficacy of the wall's piecemeal construction—where workers are tasked with building particular sections then moved across vast tracts of land to build other sections (and presumably to stave off boredom). How can a wall with holes be anything more than an invitation to invade and destroy? The story brings up the work of a scholar who has written a book attempting to prove that the wall itself, when completed, may only be the partial foundation for a biblical Tower of Babel (where, it is said, God first split humans into different language and cultural categories). The narrator goes on to relay a parable about the Emperor, who, from his own Babel-like tower in Peking, is sending a deathbed message to "the humble subject" he rules over. Due to the vast distances between city and country, between high command and rural labourer, the messenger sent to deliver the Emperor's words will never arrive at the subject's door. The "humble subject" then lives in a state of confusion and misinformation, unsure if they are ruled by one who is dead or is living, or if there is even a single emperor, or empire, to serve any longer at all.

"The Great Wall" is the centrepiece of a sequence of poems written out of Lane's experiences travelling in China. It first appeared in his 1982 collection, *Old Mother*. Consciously or not, Lane had taken up the work of Kafka's story. Both pieces are rich with empathy for unheralded workers from a faraway culture: for those workers' physical, emotional and intellectual lives. Putting aside the obvious distinctions between the functions of a stanza as opposed to a paragraph, there are key differences in terms of statements and narrative that I did not understand on first encountering the two pieces.

First of all, Kafka's narrator is at a slight remove from the day-to-day physical exertion, from the exhaustion by which Lane's speaker, tools in hand, arrives at his various moments of introspection and consideration.

A second difference is that Kafka's story describes the initial construction of the wall, while Lane's poem deals with the restorative maintenance of an existing structure. Though Lane's poem is set in the future time of Kafka's story, it is pre-modernist in how it relates to broader literary concepts of piecemeal construction and fragment. Lane's speaker does not have the luxury of moving to different sections of the wall, nor of considering the wall in states of incompletion or disrepair. Lane's speaker lives with his family at the same site for the duration of his life. He toils not just in the lack of information from his high command, but in the boredom and stasis of the work itself.

Kafka's narrator can break long enough to consider abstract concepts relating architecture to dream and empire. Lane's speaker, without time, energy, education or even memory ("They were given this work by someone / a long time ago or so his father said / but who it was he does not remember"), may require the aid of an interloper or messenger to articulate the exact nature of his doubts.

Putting the tools down, breaking from work, looking out over "the dry brown distance," Lane's speaker may consider the composition and variety of the potential landscapes and their possible correlatives to thought before "The Great Wall." Landscapes populated with intruders, with ghost stories, with the men and women of the towns where the labour is done, or merely with the unforgiving stones, fields, forests, roads and mountains in the distance.

> At that moment
> he sees between earth and sky
> a cloud of dust like the drifting spores
> of a puffball exploded by a foot.

"That moment" is an uncertain moment, possibly dreamt, possibly real. "That moment" retains both the vastness of the imaginary landscape and all the potential excitements and uncertainties the landscape sets before and conjures within the speaker. "That moment" moves backwards from modernism toward older notions of encounters with the Other, encounters that can change the course of an individual's narrative forever.

When Lane began apprenticing as a mid-twentieth-century poet, the works of sixteenth-century Flemish landscape painter Pieter Bruegel the Elder were a common well of inspiration for poets. In Sylvia Plath's "Two Views of a Cadaver Room" (from her book *The Colossus*, 1960) Lane must have found a kinship in the unflinching eye of Plath's speaker as she observes, in the first view, the heart being plucked from the cadaver of a man. So too in the second view, where the wandering, oblivious eyes of lute-playing lovers at the bottom right-hand corner of Bruegel's panoramic horror show, *The Triumph of Death*, are featured.

It is perhaps through William Carlos Williams' more clinically descriptive ekphrastic sequence, "Pictures from Brueghel" (from a book of the same title that won a Pulitzer in 1963), that Lane may have been first exposed to the rural scenes and landscapes of Bruegel's catalogue; to the peasant weddings, harvests, dances and hunting scenes that would strike a chord with the poet who would commit to describing the small-town lives in Merritt, Nelson, Vernon and Cache Creek.

Both Plath and Williams would have undoubtedly been inspired by a W.H. Auden poem from 1938, "Musée des Beaux Arts," which Patrick used in our classroom as both an example of formal eloquence and the written equivalent of nature's indifference to the suffering of man depicted in Bruegel's *Landscape with the Fall of Icarus* (which Auden's poem describes). "About suffering they were never wrong, / The old Masters" was a passage Patrick seized upon in discussion and offered to us as one of the great modern proverbs.

Bruegel embedded biblical scenes and Flemish parables into highly populated town-life paintings. He painted sequences celebrating various two-month seasons and the attendant duties and struggles of his human subjects amid vast and unforgiving landscapes. He painted winding rivers, towering trees with solitary crows on their branches, and difficult mountain passages. He captured icy winters, including Western art's first successful depiction of snowfall. He completed three paintings depicting the aforementioned Tower of Babel (one of which shows the tower dwarfing a nearby defensive wall).

While there is so much to read into the details of Bruegel's paintings, the dearth of biographical information about the painter himself enables a poet to enter his landscapes without the freight of knowledge about his cultural status or religious persuasion; about his intellectual, sexual and family life. Indeed, one is not even hindered by specific geography, as Bruegel made use of composite landscapes from both Italy and the Netherlands. He also imitated, in sometimes chillingly replicate style, some of the dreamscapes and hellscapes of the then (and still) wildly popular Hieronymus Bosch.

So prevalent were the direct references to Bruegel in the poetry reading of Lane's early apprenticeship that he might have been consciously trying to avoid referencing the painter outright. The influence had to be internalized. Lane's capacity for recreating the natural world of his youth and early manhood and conjuring the specific traumas, travails and personalities of war brides, mill workers, loggers and others could be described as Bruegelian. The influence is compositional and relates to his entire body of work. The stones pile up. Here is the literary equivalent of a Bruegel painting from Lane's memoir, *There Is a Season*:

> Two truckloads of gravel and the path is done. I sit on the
> first stone and stare down the wander of pebbles as they
> flow gently among the ferns and hostas. Where the path
> comes up against a large stone, I have tried to recreate a

stone in a stream. The pebbles slide up against the stone and then curl round it, just as water does when it meets a water stone. I sing to my path a hymn to stone.

Sea stone, water stone, stone of scree and mountain, valley stone, grass stone, outcrop, ledge and whisper stone, tooth of hill and desert, moss stone, moonstone, the many stones of this and there, vision stone, entrance stone beyond the place of bone where small lights shine with crystal stillness, hand of stone and eye of stone, knuckle stone and tongue of stone, all these and more as you walk the pebbled path, stand beside the trunk of a Douglas fir and imagine it by the sea. At your feet is a single perfect stone with striations of pale pink quartz that was your journey. You pick it up and turn and turn its many sides to your eyes in wonder. Do you remember the day you found it in the sea's wrack?

And Kafka, once more: "Yet perhaps I may venture to assert… the building of the wall in particular, with its abundance of human material, provided a man of sensibility with the opportunity of traversing the souls of almost all the provinces."

In 2009, private collectors in Spain uncovered a painting, *The Wine of Saint Martin's Day,* believed to be attributable to Pieter Bruegel the Elder. The large cloth canvas depicts the denizens of a Flemish town celebrating the Feast of Saint Martin in the typical way: that is, drinking from a gigantic barrel of the year's new vintage. The large, rich, red barrel, raised above the ground on a wooden platform, forms the centre of the painting. It is shrouded in the foreground and at its sides by the anxious hands of peasants as they reach toward the spout. Jugs, bowls, hats, even shoes are procured as drinking vessels. A young man practises pickpocketing on a woman drinking with a child affixed to her chest. The woman's older child reaches up to her waist, clutches her other hand. Another man stands underneath the raised board with his shoe toward the spout, perhaps not wanting to be seen. A man with a bowl on his head, already having had his fill, stands next to another suspicious man brandishing a large stick (probably looking to take advantage of the more compromised festival goers). The mixture of faces could be said to be more anxious than revelatory, more than a few looking sunken-eyed and desperate. A number of men ride atop the barrel, tipping their vessels downward, arms upraised and swaying with the series of treetops and chimneys at the top of the painting.

Curator of early Flemish collections Pilar Silva Maroto can walk you through the painting on the Prado's website. We are pointed toward some of the predictable consequences of excessive drinking: a man passed out, another about to vomit; two men scrapping, all hands and arms and legs; another sleeping; two more dancing; and a woman bringing a cowl to her baby's lips, perhaps "introducing the habit," as Silva suggests.

On the right side we see the titular saint on horseback, facing away from the party (suggested by historians to connote his absence from his own festival), dividing his cloak with a sword and handing the fabric down to two people, one missing his feet and legs from half shin level, the other with bowed and severely twisted legs (Bruegel being one of the first to depict without judgment people with disabilities in his scenes).

The background is more faded than in other Bruegel landscapes. This is due to the atypical application of hide-glue tempera (paint derived from animal hide) directly to linen described by its restorer as "thin... like a piece of cigarette paper," with no under-layer. But thanks to the restoration process, the shapes of a castle and its people have become clearer. Clearer too is the path, the town, the sea, a crucifix that had been completely buried under various layers of varnish, the nervous gathering of eyes at the second-floor window of a house in town, and the solitary jay, maybe a magpie, perched atop a leafless, spindly tree.

The painting, paired at the Prado with *The Triumph of Death*, was made available to the public in 2011. Leading up to that, the painstaking restoration took the better part of a year.

Much of the credit for the restoration of *The Wine of Saint Martin's Day* must go to a version of the devoted worker-poet of "The Great Wall," Elisa Mora. Over her career, she has brought a faded virgin by Titian back to life on its canvas made of marble. She has restored Titian's early paintings *Danaë* and *Venus and Adonis*, from his sequence on the origins of poetry. She was the first of the restorers to understand that Titian left certain parts of the backgrounds deliberately unpainted in order to create, in her words, "a special vibration between one plane and another." It is Mora who retransmitted "that sense of cold that Goya wanted" to his painting *The Snowstorm or Winter*. And it is Mora who brought sober clarity back to this lost masterpiece by Bruegel.

Restauradora is the job title. In two short videos on the Prado's website, Mora can be seen working on the restoration of *The Wine of Saint Martin's Day*. As she tells it, the painting underwent a series of X-rays to determine the distribution of colour and the areas of damage. Layer upon layer of polyester varnish, which had erased whole areas and images and made the painting appear as a work in oil rather than the more delicate and matted hide-glue tempera, had to be surgically removed. Then a thick relining at the back, insufficient to the task of keeping the thin linen strong (and so creating areas that bulged and sagged), had to be removed with an experimental process that involved an algae called agar-agar, used most often in the restoration of sculpture. The remaining bits of the reinforcement had to be scraped away by scalpel. After, in Mora's translated words, "we made a map of damage in order to exactly pinpoint the location of the cracks and the weakest areas in order to work particularly carefully in these zones." More than six hundred separate patches had to be remade and then individually applied to the back of the linen. Then came the fun part, "reintegrating losses to the paint surface." Mora, seen face to face with the canvas, delicately adds points from Bruegel's determined palate with her fine-tipped brush, in direct and extended conversation with the genius she attributes to the painter: "Bruegel must have been remarkably intelligent as an artist in order to locate each figure in its setting in such a complex composition," she says, clearly enamoured. "This has been a very, very, very laborious task," she concedes. And yet she is up to the job.

Her former colleague, and current director of the National Gallery in London, Gabriele Finaldi, raises "the issue of the actual restoration and the skill of the person undertaking it, given that it has to be undertaken from the surface downwards, so that the original painting is gradually revealed." It's almost shocking to see, in these and other videos, the mix of surgical, scientific exactness and the tender way the canvas moves with each slight press of the edge of Mora's hand.

Lane:

> Will they honour him for his work, the hours
> and years he has spent? ...
> No one has ever told him what would happen.

In March 2019, when I heard the news of Patrick's death, I was in Madrid. My father worked there, and my parents lived a short walk from the Prado. My routine during this trip was to leave my daughter in the care of my mother in the morning and go drink a couple of coffees downtown while reading manuscripts for my work that year as an acquisitions editor for a small Canadian publisher. The day of the news, it made sense to change my route across Retiro Park and spend an hour in front of what, in multiple museum visits over the years since it had been discovered, had come to replace its Prado roommate, *The Triumph of Death*, as my favourite painting. It made sense to sit on the bench in front of the largest work Bruegel had ever painted, with no backdrop, on the thinnest linen, using paint that's known to fade. "Paintings of this type are totally different from oil paintings," Mora says, "and have to be seen with fresh eyes."

When his head fell on the open page that first day of class, I was struck by the weight of Patrick's statement—"and it's all you fucking have." I was asking to be struck, and for a long time I did not care if the dizziness of that blow prevented me from seeing what a world is.

Patrick was in recovery. What I was able to watch in the early years of his recovery was the new openness in his interactions with students, the new vulnerability in his own poems and in his beautiful memoir.

So after my time with *The Wine of Saint Martin's Day*, I sat on a bench in Retiro Park. A small bird was flitting in a tree. I was reminded of the wasp Patrick saw, and also the crow that acknowledged Patrick while holding the wasp down with its claws. I imagined a painter, shaking, who could no longer hold their brush. And I was grateful to Patrick for whatever had been removed in the late, bright years of his listening.

LUNCH HOUR

It was the best poetry reading I'd ever been to.
Noon start. Poem after poem
after poem, and no banter. Like being
at a dinner party full of incisive guests. More food
and wine than anyone could handle. Slaps
on the back and laughter, laughter...
But it was just Tomaž Šalamun reading
twenty poems in thirty minutes;
one thousand poems
in thirty minutes—for all of us, at lunch.

NOTES

Information about the Indigenous cultural references in the essay "If It Gets Quiet Later On, I Will Make a Display" were checked against the *Wolastoqiyik and Mi'kmaq Studies Elementary Level Handbook*, available online at www.wabanakicollection.com.

"Cool Clouds on a Drive," "A John Ashbery Remembrance Day," "The Apartment Above the Shop" and "Lunch Hour" appeared previously in a chapbook from Anstruther Press, *The Cloud from All Sides* (2021); my thanks to editor Jim Johnstone. "A John Ashbery Remembrance Day" and "Small Talk" first appeared in *The Ampersand Review* (Issue No. 1, summer 2021); my thanks to editor Paul Vermeersch.

"Book It" is a work of fiction.

"Librería Gloria Fuertes" is a work of fiction. The quoted passages from Gloria Fuertes are from the anthology *Roots and Wings: Poetry from Spain, 1900–1975* (Harper & Row, 1976), edited by Hardie St. Martin and translated by Philip Levine.

"Protocol" is a work of fiction.

"Collected Trout" is an essay produced in consultation and conversation with all three of the Trouts, and was originally published online in *Forget Magazine* (July 2017); my thanks to editor Kent Bruyneel.

"Freshet and Long Cross" is a work of fiction. Nevertheless, a number of characters are inspired by individuals from the Wolastoqey Nation: in particular, members of the Brooks family of Sitansisk/St. Mary's Wolastoqiyik First Nation who make and repair traditional canoes, and the Tobique First Nation member Jeremy Dutcher, an internationally successful musician and composer. It is my sincere hope that, while a work of fiction, this story honours the profound and ongoing cultural contributions of those indigenous to this corner of Turtle Island. Thank you. *Woliwon*.

In my fictionalized essay "Notes on a Version of *The Waste Land*" I have called the translator F because I understand that my perspective is incomplete, subjective and therefore fictitious. I have used his full name where I quote his own translation. I endeavoured to track Fernando Vargas down prior to publication of this piece, but was unsuccessful. The quoted passages are from *The Letters of T.S. Eliot, Volume 1: 1898–1922* (Houghton Mifflin Harcourt, 1988), edited by Valerie Eliot, and T.S. Eliot's *Collected Poems 1909–1962* (Faber, 1974).

"Epilogue Books" is a work of fiction. The quoted passages and story described therein are from *Bibliomania* by Gustave Flaubert (Rodale Press, 1954).

"The Gaffer and the Morning Star" is a work of fiction.

"Goodbye, Great Wall" is an essay that was first published in *Brick: A Literary Journal* (Issue 109, summer 2022). Thanks to editors Laurie D. Graham, Liz Johnston, Allison LaSorda and Orly Zebak for their care and attention to this piece.

ACKNOWLEDGEMENTS

For financial assistance that made the writing of this book possible, I wish to thank the Canada Council for the Arts (2020), Arts NB (2018) and the Calgary Distinguished Writers Program (2015–2016).

Thanks to the colleagues and dear ones who read all or parts of the manuscript, offering suggestions, clarifications, collaborations: Lorna Crozier, Degan Davis, Raoul Fernandes, Jeffrey Gustavson, Matthew Gwathmey, Drew Kennickell, Kalpna Patel, Rob Taylor, the Old Trout Puppet Workshop (Pete Balkwill, Judd Palmer and Steve "Pityu" Kenderes) and Chris Wilson-Smith. Thanks to Paige Cooper for the kind words on the cover. Thanks to Emma Skagen, Karine Hack, Carleton Wilson and everyone else at Nightwood Editions. Thanks, as ever, to Sue Sinclair.

Gratitude as well to my employers and colleagues past and present at Westminster Books in Fredericton, Book City in Bloor West Village (Toronto) and Book City in the Danforth (Toronto). And to the staff and patrons of independent bookstores everywhere.

PHOTO CREDIT: DREW GILBERT

ABOUT THE AUTHOR

Nick Thran is the author of three collections of poems. His second collection, *Earworm* (Nightwood Editions, 2011), won the Trillium Book Award for Poetry. After stops in Toronto, Victoria, New York, Calgary, Madrid and Montreal, he now lives in Fredericton, New Brunswick, on the unceded and unsurrendered territory of the Wolastoqiyik, where he also works as an editor and bookseller.